SCIENCE IN THE SÉANCE ROOM

by

PAUL MILLER

REPRINTED FROM
PSYCHIC BOOK CLUB EDITIONS
VOLUMES I & II (1945)

Published by
Saturday Night Press Publications
England.
snppbooks@gmail.com
www.snppbooks.com

ISBN 978-1-908421-32-6

Printed and distributed by
by Lightning Source
www.lightningsource.com

Cover Design: Ann Harrison@SNPPbooks. Background from the original wartime cover with added images of the scientists included the book: Clockwise from top right : A. Russel Wallace; Prof. Robt. Hare; Sir Oliver Lodge; Sir Wm. F. Barratt; Dr W.J. Crawford; Dr R.J. Tillyard; Dr Charles Richet; Prof. J.C.F. Zöllner; Prof. James Mapes; Sir Wm. Crookes and illustrations (front & back) from Sir William Crookes' *Researches into Spiritualism* (1926).

PREFACE FROM THE PUBLISHER

It is a privilege to be able to bring this book about our pioneer researchers back into print. So much has been said over the years that they were too specialised in their individual areas of expertise, or too old, to be able to see clearly if they were being duped by charlatans. Not so!

In these pages Paul Miller details not only the breadth of their scientific expertise in many areas but quotes from the records they kept of their researches into aspects of the supra-normal phenomena they witnessed—not on one or two occasions but in some cases over many years.

Throughout history, contact with the 'Other World' has always been there but as the Western World descended into Materialism in the 19th Century an effort was made by the Spirit World to keep that contact going. To make the inhabitants of this 'Brave New World' aware that there was more than the "here and now" and it was important to build spiritual progression into our lives.

In those early days of the mid 1800s the only way to get the attention of the people was by creating supra-normal physical happenings – 'rappings' and 'tappings' on whatever they could; movement and levitation of heavy objects beyond what a conjuror/magician could achieve; musical instruments that appeared to 'play themselves' and messages spelled out, which could only have come intelligence beyond this physical world.

As the years pass it is vital that we do not forget the research into things 'psychical' done by those to whom it was a whole new experience. This book, written over seventy years ago, details the work, and the standing, of some of the most prominent of those scientists who applied their experimental methods to this research and came up with the conclusion there was more to life than "meets the eye".

I have had Volume II of this war-time book in my collection for many years. Now at last I have been able to marry it up with Volume I from the bookshelves of Karl Jackson-Barnes, who has graciously scanned it for me.

So from the two of us, we give you this wonderful account of our Pioneers, not this time of the Mediums, but of those who observed their work, and the efforts of the Spirit World, to turn us from the pursuit solely of Materialism to a more balanced life in which our material pursuits could benefit Mankind and advance our own spiritual growth.

I quote from Lord Dunraven's work on his sittings with D.D.Home in 1870[1]. "It is remarkable that this new source of evidence should be discovered at a time when materialism, and the denial of a future state are on the increase, apparently in all parts of the world, and are said to prevail to an alarming extent in America, the country, be it remarked, where first these manifestations occurred on a large or striking scale. The timidity or apathy of men of science in England on this subject is to be deplored."

Nothing has changed! I recently spoke to a young tutor at my local University who said, "I can't believe in it – I'm a scientist."

I replied, "So were Sir William Crookes, Sir Oliver Lodge and Sir William Barrett."

The Spirit World must be wringing their hands after all their efforts over 170 years since the "Hydesville Rappings" took America by storm.

---

1. Adare, Viscount. *Experiences in Spiritualism with D.D.Home*. White Crow Books. Kindle Edition.

So here again—in hope—is Paul Miller's book, first published in 1945—under war-time restrictions, with the details of those and seven other pioneer scientists who were diligent in their researches.

I have also decided to add diagrams of some of the apparatus devised by these scientists for their experiments on the front and back covers, and at the end of the book are the two advertising pages from the end of Volume II, showing what other books were available at that time under "Psychic Press Publications"—a little more of the history of the time for you, which is also reflected in the bluff brown colour of the cover – again wartime restrictions, "lest we forget".

Ann Harrison
November 2018

CONTENTS

FOREWORD

SPIRITUALISM is the only religion the fundamentals of which can be scientifically proved. All other religions, whatever their antiquity, no matter how novel they may be, lack the support of proved and tested facts from which can be inferred the operation of natural laws, which in their scope and magnitude offer to mankind a conception of the universe perfectly ruled and ideally balanced.

In other times men worshipped the unexplained phenomena of nature and cowered before the operation of forces which they could neither understand nor admit to examination since they themselves were ignorant. In later times tribal deities and gods hold the world in a prison-house state of fear. Not even the most powerful religions today can produce testifiable facts in support of the dogmas and creeds with which they hold sway over millions of people, who in any other field of activity would demand knowledge as a basis of faith and works as proof of validity of assertions.

But this Spiritualism, in less than a century, has been tested more than almost any other proposition affecting mankind. With each new inquiry a new controversy has been begun; as each prominent convert stood forth boldly to declare the truth of what he himself had discovered by personal investigation of facts, a new wave of scorn, prejudice, bitterness and opposition has dashed against him. These eminent men and women who courageously testified to the fundamental truths of Spiritualism have passed on, and it is largely from their record that I draw the material for this book. No apology is needed for this because we are of a world fellowship, the only difference being that I am not a scientist and they no longer inhabit physical bodies. But we have a common task to present to all who care to read facts, experiences, records and, in short, a body of truth the like of which has never before been so constantly pressed forward for humanity's attention.

It is natural that as time passes even great figures are forgotten, reputations that were once universal fade into the mists, the books that in their day created a stir become the inhabitants of ageing libraries and collect the dust of years. But the truth which is recorded in the lives of the great scientists and others who have boldly declared what they proved to be truth is ammunition in a great war against prejudice, ignorance and fear of the new.

There is no scientist, no author, no lawyer, no man or woman of public force who has set out upon this inquiry and later proclaimed conviction, who has not been assailed. That is one fact emerging clearly from the preparation of the material. Men of national and international reputation have been driven from positions of importance, others have been compelled to resign, all because they said they had proved it was true that the human soul survives death, that in the right conditions the living and the dead communicate, that the dead persist, with all their faculties heightened, and in some cases extended, ready, willing and eager to co-operate with those they have left behind. These great inquirers, these pioneers, have found to be established, as certainly as the law of gravity is established, that the psychic phenomena of Spiritualism can be exhibited, proving that there are laws in nature of which men are not yet master; that there are powers which in a physical body they cannot, so far, control, and that when we pass hence we are bound still by the ties of love to those among whom we lived.

No one man or woman in this affair stands out before another. It was given to some to have greater scientific reputations, but each according to his position has given of his best. To a few, conviction came speedily, some laboured for years, even as many as twenty, to find at last those clinching pieces of evidence which made them certain and brave enough to stand forth before the sceptical and rightly doubting world to tell all they knew and found to be true.

The list is long, the names are illustrious and the facts they have found are of such a character that they have changed world thought in the course of one century. Yet they have not changed the whole world as much as was hoped, but have been a leavening process, in that ancient untruths and manufactured creeds and dogmas which held sway a hundred years ago are now almost wholly neglected, except by those who have by profession to proclaim them and by those whose eyes are blinkered from truth.

It has often been asked by sceptics, why there is not a university of Spiritualism, and why there is not one indisputable test that can be repeated again and again so that the doubter may be convinced against his will, the Rationalist persuaded beyond his reason, the ordinary man stimulated to a believing state of wonder and the prejudiced divided in his loyalty even to his fears. But this could not be, for all men differ and to each is given that evidence, that phenomena, that experience and that wisdom which he earns for himself. No man can receive knowledge beyond his understanding; no one will accept what in the end is not acceptable to his reason; therefore, there could be no universal test. This is a personal religion which, in total, embraces all men on this earth. For as many as have inquired, there was as many stories of searches, seances, experience, expectations fulfilled, hopes disappointed, doubts, questions and, in the end, that satisfaction which makes the honest human being say, "Now I know it is true!"

If it were otherwise, of course, the subject of Spiritualism would not argue, and debate would be ended, doubt would disappear, and so would this truth. There are no longer flaming controversies about the creeds and dogmas for which, in unhappier times, many were sent to the stake and to the tomb for some denied faiths they knew to be untrue and therefore untenable. Those who were witnesses of this truth of the spirit, which I now here espouse, were subject to the vilest tortures that men can devise, and that system whereby progress is strangled has not wholly died from this world to this day.

This is not the first time that efforts have been made to establish for the use of all men a knowledge of the spirit, of its gifts, and of the manifold uses to which it can be put for the reforming of the world. This is the mission of Spiritualism to reform the whole world and found it on a spiritual basis; because man, being a spirit in systems which operate on the assumption that he is otherwise, this denial of his spiritual faculties must produce oppression which leads to a slavery and to an autocracy which leads to decay.

No tolerant person can survey the world today and say that he is satisfied with what is being done, what is being taught and what is being planned for the future of mankind. Any system of society, to endure and be just, cannot disregard the spiritual nature of man which is so powerful yet so sensitive that it requires patience and much effort to understand it. Here exhibited in the records of those who have proved many thousands of times that what I say is true are instances of intelligence, forethought, consideration and love, showing that in spiritual form man is much the same as he is in his physical body, with this exception only – that he has greater freedom of movement and can more readily find knowledge on which to base his actions.

As the creeds and the dogmas, religious and political, have become weakened, as spiritual knowledge advances, there has been left between the two contending forces a vast body of dissenters who have cared little one way or the other which way the battle went, but its outcome must affect them all, for in time this knowledge will become part of the equipment of every human being. It may be generations, it may be centuries but a time will come, as certainly as these words are written, when the knowledge of the gifts of the spirit will be universal.

The unconvinced could argue, and with some reason, that if, in earlier decades, outstanding scientists were convinced of the truths of Spiritualism and said so, why have they not been universally accepted? The answer is that progress is not made only by violent revolution. When the scientists and the experimenters had done their duty they passed on, and new generations had to learn for themselves all that these pioneers had found. That is what happens in schools, in colleges and in universities. Because one man proved the existence of the law of gravity it did not mean that that knowledge was thereby automatically conferred upon every human being possessed of a brain. Each generation has to seek its own proof, conduct its own controversy and find its own satisfaction – or lack of it.

This great campaign, of which we are but a small part, was not intended to be won by one revolt, by one scientist or by one prominent convert. It is difficult, in writing, to recapture the thrill of evidence witnessed at first hand. When the voice speaks and the hand moves, when an object is lifted by a spiritual power, when a materialised form speaks again in a well-loved voice, no words from any pen can set it down. That is why this living knowledge is best found by every man for himself.

A review of the evidence presented by scientists fascinates me who ought by now to have been hardened by hundreds of psychic experiences. But each one is different, and that is not my testimony alone but the verdict of hundreds who have established for themselves what men of the calibre of Russel Wallace, Barrett, Lodge, Fichte, Zöllner, Mapes, Flammarion, Hare, Elliotson and de Morgan have found. This in itself should indicate to the perceptive mind that there are intelligences behind the phenomena, for it could not be by accident that men of such critical abilities should have found each for himself sufficient evidence to bring personal conviction. Most of them inquired in their own homes, and in a few cases in scientific laboratories, but all in circumstances in which there could be no suggestion that they were deceived, that they were a party to deception or that they were mistaken.

If this subject had been investigated by one man, that argument might have had point, but when, as I will show, inquiries have been conducted in the leading civilised countries, and that all the experiences resulted in the same conclusions, then it must be conceded that the case is proved.

There is no test, even to the point of cruelty, which has not been imposed on mediums. They have been bound hand and foot, they have been gagged, their feet have been held, their hands have been gripped, they have been blindfolded, they have been placed in cages – and yet the phenomena persisted. It has been proved that, with certain types of mediums, psychic force can move and lift heavy objects without physical contact. It has been established beyond doubt that this force is not a freak of electricity. It has been proved that, in the right conditions, fully-formed materialisations can walk, talk, dance and even eat, can reason and bring evidence in their own well-loved voices to prove that they are who they say they are.

When all prejudice has been set aside, when all ignorant scoffing has been stilled, these facts remain. It is not done by sleight of hand, it is not done by regurgitation, it is not done by mass hypnotism, it is not done by suggestion, it is not done by emanation of the brain; nothing of this is the operation of so called secondary personalities, it is not done by demons, by lying spirits, by necromancy, witchcraft, wizardry, or the occult arts. The facts are achieved solely by the co-operation of the living and the dead. From the ranks of the vast armies of this world some are chosen because they are mediums. That is to say, they are the custodians of spiritual gifts which can be developed so that, in concert with more experienced souls who are different only because they do not have physical bodies, there can be displayed for all who are interested the phenomena on which this religion of Spiritualism bases its physical, evidential proof.

It is as simple as any honest, comprehensive, universal truth can be. The marvel is that so much has been done and that so much prejudice persists. But side by side with conviction in high places and testimony of the learned and the distinguished, there has emerged a bitter and unrelenting opposition to those who have vested interests of the mind to serve. When all the scientists have brought forth their testimony, when all the experiences have been declared, when all the remarkable phenomena have been attested and the search begun for the underlying laws, there remains the fact that this truth was not intended as a scientific experiment alone. It was brought into the world again that the whole world might share in its benefits.

It was, and is, intended to heal the broken heart and body, to increase understanding, to illuminate the mind, to spread tolerance, to encourage a love of justice and to promote that true feeling of brotherhood without which all things are in vain.

The contribution of the scientists has been a great one; they nobly served what they knew to be true. It is for us to make use of their testimony, their conviction and their brave acts to encourage the nameless millions of this world to inquire for themselves and to seek healing, comfort and understanding.

There is no country in the world where this truth in some form has not been demonstrated; some lands have been more fortunate than others in that they have produced groups of men and women who more readily seized on the value and power of this teaching. The service which Spiritualists and the spirit people who support them have rendered to humanity in less than a hundred years cannot be computed because we who journey through it cannot see the whole effect of an idea upon the world.

Many were known and famed in their own day. Others laboured in barren obscurity and their example shines through centuries. Which of the two is the more valuable servant of humanity? It is not my business to determine this issue, but it is a duty and pleasure to record that many have left comfort and ease, the beaten ways of orthodoxy and the normal passage towards preferment, to champion a cause that they could easily have neglected. Some were driven to this truth, others were driven by it. Few of the scientists whose works I will summarise have come to it as a result of personal grief. To almost all it was a scientific subject scientifically approached and the result has been such a magnificence of testimony that if it could be but presented to the millions it must have a tremendous effect.

CHAPTER ONE

HIS SCEPTICISM WAS VANQUISHED

ALFRED RUSSEL WALLACE, co-discoverer with Darwin of the theory of natural selection, is one of that band of English scientists who flourished in an atmosphere first of academism, then rational unbelief, until he was driven by facts to state that he was convinced of Spiritualism. "I am well aware," he wrote, "that my scientific friends are somewhat puzzled to account for what they consider to be my delusion and believe that it has injuriously affected whatever power I may have once possessed of dealing with the philosophy of natural history."

To answer criticisms that his beliefs were due to religious or clerical prejudice, he makes this answer: "From the age of 14, I lived with an elder brother, of advanced philosophical and religious opinions, and I soon lost, and have never since regained, all capacity of being affected in my judgments, either by clerical influence or religious prejudice." Before he was confronted by the facts of Spiritualism he was a philosophical sceptic. He delighted in Voltaire, and to the end remained an admirer of Herbert Spencer. He was such a materialist that a spiritual conception of the universe was almost repugnant to him. The world, he thought, was ruled by matter and force. And this is how he began to change his mind.

Some slight psychic phenomena occurred in a friend's family and Wallace's curiosity was so stimulated that he began to inquire. The facts became quickly varied and so far removed from what the science of his day taught that their attraction became irresistible. He accepted these facts long before he was convinced of their explanation. At first, he could not assimilate this new knowledge into his system of philosophy, but little by little it found a place for itself. And now, at the risk of wearying the reader a little, I will try to show that in his case—and it could be true of all the others—he was not wholly unprepared for what was to happen to him. For he says that he was following a "strictly logical and scientific course in seeing how far this doctrine [of the existence of intelligences other than human and capable of influencing human minds] can account for some of those residual phenomena which natural selection alone will not explain."

His book, *Contribution to the Theory of Natural Selection,* has a chapter in which he deals with what he called "residual phenomena"—that is, phenomena not covered by the general theory; or what is left over when a scientist has done theorising and what he had to admit he cannot explain. In that book on natural history, Russel Wallace says he suggested that these residual phenomena may be due to the "action of some of the various intelligences." He stated that opinion long before he knew of Spiritualism. He realised when he wrote that it was difficult to demonstrate, but after he became a Spiritualist he said, "I still maintain it is one which is logically tenable and is in no way inconsistent with a thorough acceptance of the grand doctrine of evolution through natural selection, although implying—as indeed many of the chief supporters of that doctrine admit that it is not the all-powerful, all-sufficient and only cause of the development of organic forms."

That is somewhat heavy reading, but the point is this—that this seeker after truth was honestly stating a scientific difficulty in which he was placed by facts unexplainable by the current theory. And this is how he obtained conviction, this is how, in the séance room, he found that body of knowledge which helped to explain the residual phenomena which the theory of natural selection could not make clear. Russel Wallace's story is not one of retorts and test tubes, of gauges and measures, of spring balances or micrometers. Even before the birth of modern Spiritualism he was interested in psychic phenomena.

In 1843 a controversy was raging in London over the work of Dr Elliotson, an outstanding Spiritualist, who with other surgeons had performed operations on patients while they were in mesmeric trance. Wallace found himself observing that the medical authorities of the day said either that the mesmerised patients were impostors or were naturally insensible to pain. The operating surgeons were even accused of bribing these patients. Dr Elliotson was branded as a heretic, he had polluted the temple of science, and orthodox science, in its zeal for the conventional, opposed the reading of a paper by him describing an amputation during magnetic trance. The result—Dr Elliotson was thrown out of his professorship in the University of London. That was a phenomenon of an order not uncommon in these days. It impressed Russel Wallace but did not diminish his interest.

Then he heard a mesmerist give a lecture and was assured by him that any healthy person could mesmerise his friends and reproduce the phenomena demonstrated on the platform during the lecture. Wallace tried and he found he was a good mesmerist.

He says: "I thus learned my first great lesson in the inquiry into these obscure fields of knowledge, never to accept the disbelief of great men, of their accusations of imposture or imbecility as of any weight as opposed to the repeated observation of facts by other men admittedly sane and honest. The whole history of science shows us that, whenever the educated and scientific men of any age have denied the facts of investigators on *a priori* grounds of absurdity or impossibility, they have always been wrong."

Although Elliotson had to lose his job to prove a fact and mesmerism was declared to be an imposture, a few years later it was admitted to be true. Those who had denied its truth soon had proved to them that even more remarkable phenomena including clairvoyance, occurred in the presence of human beings. Russel Wallace became acquainted with the researches of Baron von Reichenbach, the much scoffed-at investigator who established the existence of the aura around all objects. The scientist has to admit that phenomena which puzzles the scientific world of his day, were understood and explained by the so-called uneducated masses, but for a reason he does not explain, that is many of them held their own home circles and witnessed psychic happenings under conditions as favourable as those of any one I shall mention in this book.

To the jibe or the criticism that Spiritualism does not present a scientific theory of life Wallace answers with this: "For myself, I have never been able to see why any one hypothesis should be less scientific than another, except so far as one explains the whole of the facts, and the other explains only a part of them. I therefore claim that the spirit hypothesis is the most scientific since even those who oppose it most strenuously often admit that it has explained all the facts, which cannot be said under any other hypothesis."

When Wallace experimented in mesmerism, he found he could produce "partial or complete catalepsy, paralysis of the motor-nerves in certain directions, or of any special sense, any kind of delusion by suggestion, insensibility to pain, and community of sensation with myself when at a considerable distance from the patient. All this was demonstrated in such a number of patients, and under such varied conditions, as to satisfy me of the genuineness of the phenomena." Thus it can be seen that this scientist had a good basis for his inquiry because he had practical experience. He proved for himself by experiment to be true what other scientists of his day without investigation had denied as being contrary to the laws of nature.

But he never accepted, to his last day on earth, that men had even approached a complete understanding of the laws of nature. He believed firmly in the aphorism that when a fact emerges contrary to accepted belief it should be eagerly seized on as pointing the way to a new truth. He quotes the instance of one French naturalist informing another that he had reared perfect silkworms from eggs laid by a virgin moth. The reply was that it was impossible; therefore, it was disbelieved. Yet Wallace comments that though it was contrary to "one of the widest and best established laws of nature, it is now universally admitted to be true, and the supposed law ceases to be universal."

He takes the stand that illustrations of that kind lead us to understand how alleged miracles may be due to laws of nature still undiscovered, saying: "We know so little of what nerve or life force really is, how it acts or can act, and in what degree it is capable of transmission from one human being to another, that it would be indeed rash to affirm that under no exceptional conditions could phenomena such as the apparently miraculous cure of many diseases, of perception through other channels than the ordinary senses, ever take place."

Since that statement was made, millions of instances of perception through non-physical channels have been given. Mediums all over the world, in the course of their service, have established the existence of psychic and spiritual faculties, have perceived objects and events far removed from them in time and place. Still other mediums, healers, have cured of the most painful diseases people whom they could not see and whom they did not know, because they were at the other end of the world.

It is very easy to understand how and why one with long training in orthodox science or medicine should resist with the full power of his critical faculties such a body of evidence. Teaching in schools, experiments in clinics and operating theatres, long observation in laboratories, plus the positive affirmations of materialist philosophers would lead any man or woman to a firm belief that, if the boundary of knowledge had not been reached, at least what had been established could not be overthrown.

Yet the boundaries of knowledge can never be reached.

It is when the new fact, of which Wallace thought so much, emerges that the trouble begins. The first reaction of the conventional and commonplace mind, and even of distinguished minds, is of furious resistance to the intruder. All invasions of the human consciousness are at first resented. Few of us in this world go about openly seeking new truths and new ideas, fully aware that when they are discovered our whole mode of thought will be changed. Deep in every human heart there is a yearning for the safety and comfort of some one idea, of a concept which will establish for ever a line of conduct that will lead to happiness. But progress is not made that way. We rise only with difficulty and fall to rise again, strengthened by experience and with a firmer character and a greater capacity for perceiving one more truth at a time.

It is very easy to see, by casting your mind back into Wallace's day, when the whole world was surging forward on a wave of material progress, how difficult it was for those in the spirit world charged with the mission of making the first inroads. Yet, because materialism was at its most powerful, and seemed all dominating, it was the more necessary for the great work to begin. For this truth to have found lodgement in the mind of an outstanding naturalist such as Wallace was indeed a triumph of skill and unseen direction, for I cannot see that his conviction and life-long championship of this revolutionary idea could have been achieved other than by careful endeavour persistently carried out. You can, if you choose, trace the threads back to his boyhood and see how his sceptical environment was the best preparation for his calm consideration of psychic things.

It has been found in this work that a form of agnosticism is, for most people, the best introduction. Where orthodox religious training has become associated with emotion and sentiment, and the whole is fused with a high standard of personal conduct, there is but one incident that will startle the mind from the comfort of its seclusion. That is death, which is the great teacher, the unfailing guide, the friend and the philosopher who comes to us all in time, pointing in the silence of our grief to the fact that we do not yet know sufficient to remain calm and undisturbed in the face of natural events. But Wallace was not of this order; he was exceptional, and that is why I have chosen him as a representative man out of a great band of those who proved Spiritualism to be true, in spite of the opposition of his day, and in face of the temptation to be content with what he already knew.

Phrenology is not so popular as it was, say, fifty or sixty years ago. Briefly, it is the theory that mental faculties and powers are associated with particular areas in the brain and that delineation of qualities can be done from the configuration of the skull. Now, Wallace was interested in phrenology. It arose from his interest in mesmerism. He used the one to help him to understand the other. With the ardour of youth, he carried out many experiments in mesmerism, making sure to exclude deception, and test for himself the nature of mesmeric influence. When he was a mature man, assured of fame in the world of science, those mesmeric and phrenological experiments were stamped vividly on his memory. He produced quite easily the trance state in boys aged from twelve to sixteen. He was sure the trances were genuine because he turned the eyeball in the orbit so that the pupil was not visible when the eyelid was raised. He noticed the characteristic change of countenance, and also how easily he could produce catalepsy and loss of sensation in any part of the body.

Catalepsy means the sudden suspension of voluntary sensation, and by inducing it the experimenter is then able to excite the sensations he chooses. This is what Wallace did. He placed his finger on the part of the head corresponding to a given phrenological organ, and of the results he says: "The corresponding faculty was manifested with wonderful and amusing perfection. For a long time I thought that the effects produced on the patient were caused by my wishing the particular manifestation, but I found by accident that when, by ignorance of the position of the organs, I placed my finger on the wrong part, the manifestation which followed was not that which I expected, but that which was due to the position touched.

"I was particularly interested in phenomena of this kind, and by experiments made alone and silently, completely satisfied myself that the effects were not due to suggestion or to the influence of my own mind. I had to buy a little phrenological bust for my own use, and none of the boys had the least knowledge of, or taste for, phrenology. Yet, from the very first, almost all the organs touched, in however varied order and in perfect silence, were followed by manifestations too striking to be mistaken, and presenting more wonderful representations of varied phrases of human feeling than the greatest actors are able to exhibit."

All this is given to illustrate the development of Wallace's mind and to show that he proceeded carefully by the experimental method. In his own words he had described a scientific experiment. The results were convincing, the ideas unpopular— in his time—and I do not know whether they are any more popular today.

As he continued his experiments he says he made this discovery: "The sympathy of sensation between my patient and myself was to me the most mysterious phenomenon I had ever witnessed. I found when I had hold of his hand, he felt, tasted, or smelt exactly as I did. I had already produced all the phenomena of suggestion, and could make him tipsy with a glass of water by calling it brandy, and cause him to strip off all his clothes by telling him he was on fire." Those statements ought to cause a good deal of disbelief. But before casting them aside you should remember who said them.

Wallace began life as an architect, turned to botany, became a schoolmaster, and in 1848, the year in which Spiritualism was born in America, he set out for the River Amazon on a botanical expedition. On the return journey a large part of his collection was destroyed in a fire aboard ship. From 1854 to 1862, he was in the Malay Archipelago, where he did considerable work on zoology. His own researches, and his study of the views of Malthus, led him to formulate the idea of the "survival of the fittest." Few phrases have been so well worked by the materialist as that one, and you might as well know now that the man who first evolved it became a Spiritualist.

But this theory of the survival of the fittest was co-related to natural selection. This led Wallace to formulate the law that every species originates at the same time and in the same locality as a pre-existing closely allied species. He wrote immediately to Darwin, who received the letter on June 18, 1858. Darwin noted the extraordinary coincidence of Wallace's views and his own and communicated with Sir C. Lyell, the famous geologist, and Sir Joseph Hooker on the same day. As a result, a joint Russel Wallace-Darwin paper was read to the Linnean Society on July 1, 1858. Wallace's great scientific work, *Contributions to the Theory of Natural Selection*, was published in 1871 and contained his views on evolution, differing in points from those set forth by Darwin. Wallace's difference is that he insists on "a spiritual influence in man's development," thus departing clearly from what is called the realm of pure science, which means, of course, materialism.

He was awarded the Royal Medal in 1868 and was the first recipient of the Darwin Medal in 1890 from the Royal Society. He was honoured by Oxford University, and received a state pension through Gladstone's influence. That is a summary of the work of the man whose experiments in mesmerism and phrenology did not in any way prevent the development of his mind to that point where he stands, at least, on an equal footing with Darwin and shows, by his ready acceptance of new facts which contradicted accepted theories, that he had a more original mind. That is, he had a mind constantly seeking new principles, and it is the discoverer of the principle, particularly of a first principle, who stands first and foremost among the pioneers of thought and discovery.

Wallace's Spiritualism was not popular with his fellow scientists. Biographies of him in reference books almost scoff at his psychic experiences. But why should he have been deterred by any conventional notion of what a scientist should or should not do? He was interested in truth, and if he could discover it through phrenology, mesmerism, or any other ism or ology he had the courage to say so.

Of his experiments in phrenology and mesmerism, he says: "I formed a chain of several persons, at one end of which was the patient, at the other, myself. And when, in perfect silence, I was pinched or pricked, he would immediately put his hand to a corresponding part of his own body and complain of being pinched or pricked, too. If I put a lump of salt or sugar in my mouth, he immediately went through the action of sucking, and showed by gestures and words what it was I was tasting. I have never to this day been satisfied with any explanation given for this fact by our physiologists – for they resolve themselves into this, that the boy neither felt nor tasted anything, but acquired a knowledge of what I was feeling and tasting by a preternatural acuteness of hearing. That he had any such preternatural acuteness was, however, contrary to all my experience, and the experiment was tried to prevent his gaining any knowledge of what I felt or touched by the means of the ordinary senses."

Wallace's experience with those opposed to his conclusions in these experiments is common. When confronted with anything new or different, the first move is to find fault with the experimenter. If he has an established position, and is master of the experimental method, then a new line of criticism has to be sought. If the experiment is not faulty and the experimenter is unassailable, then it must be something else. The experimenter who is a Spiritualist is never given the benefit of any doubt. And, in the end, an explanation is brought forward which, from the materialist point of view, is more fantastic than the new facts which the Spiritualist-scientist has put forward. In this case, Wallace has explained that he made the experiments in silence, and how silence by the experimenter leads to "preternatural hearing" by the mesmeric subject is not clear. Assuming, for the sake of argument, that the materialistic explanation is right and that the mesmerised patient had developed abnormal hearing, by what means could he distinguish between the sound produced on the tongue by a lump of salt and a piece of sugar? To explain that phenomenon would be a feat.

Wallace discovered in the course of his experiments that as the boys were mesmerised more frequently during their ordinary waking conditions he could easily induce catalepsy. His observations showed that it was a real and not an imaginary state that resulted. Once, in his room, a boy was in a cataleptic state completely rigid. Then the dinner bell rang. Quickly the scientist made the necessary mesmeric pass to relax the fixed condition of the body and the limbs, and together they went down to dinner. When food was put in front of the boy, he found that one arm would not bend. He was embarrassed, did not say anything, but glanced appealingly at Wallace, who went to him, made a few passes, restored him to a normal condition and then the boy ate his dinner. The scientist makes this comment, that the important fact is that this lad thought he was all right, tried to move his arm and found he could not. He expected to be normal and found he was not. If the materialistic explanation of suggestion were true, then the lad's expectation of ability to move his arm ought to have enabled him to do so. But it did not, and a mesmeric pass was required to release him.

Over this boy and another, Wallace had such complete control that could easily produce temporary loss of any sense, such as hearing or smelling. He could deprive them of memory to such an extent that they did not know their own names and they were confused and even disgusted when he asked them to recall them. Then Wallace would make a pass across the face of a boy and say in an ordinary tone, "Now you know your name again," and the whole countenance would change, showing relief as memory returned and the familiar words were repeated. Regretfully Wallace reported that these phenomena were accepted as happening, not as the result of a trick, but were explained away by "suggestion" and "abstraction" and were denied a place in scientific knowledge.

CHAPTER TWO

SPIRIT EXPLAINS MAGNETISM

WHAT bearing has all this on Spiritualism? Here are the words of a spirit guide spoken through Cora Tappan, an outstanding trance medium, in London in 1873: "Animal magnetism, as it is called, is that peculiar force that emanates from one human body and has its influence over another human body. All substances are surrounded by magnetic properties peculiarly their own. The human body is surrounded by a magnetic element peculiarly its own."

That is to say, everybody and everything has a magnetic aura the existence of which has already been noted and experimentally established by von Reichenbach. The spirit lecturer continues:

"This element has nothing to do with the will, volition, desire, or other mental attributes of the person. It is purely a physical magnetism. It acts, reacts and otherwise operates unconsciously, and whoever possesses the most of this aura or magnetism has the most physical power and influence, and when it is accompanied by corresponding mental vigour it produces what is known as mesmerism. Mesmerism is the result of this same magnetism under the control of an individual, distinct and absolute will power. When a person wishes to mesmerise another, he avails himself of this magnetic aura that surrounds himself, and it is always the person possessing the strongest magnetic aura that can by his will power control another who has less positive will power. The other may have as much magnetism, but not having the will power to direct it he cannot resist the superior force of the mesmerist."

Now we can appreciate what Wallace discovered. It was revolutionary, but it was neglected. Because of that neglect, science, and therefore mankind, had lost a body of knowledge to which it is rightly entitled. Clearly this knowledge, properly applied, could be a curative agent, especially in mental troubles. The sceptic is entitled to ask by what authority does this spirit lecturer speak. Simply this—he is a spirit, he operates on his medium by the means he has outlined; therefore he has the required authority. The same spirit guide speaks again: "Now this mesmeric control is governed by absolute, distinctive laws under the influence of mind, and it is known that certain portions of the human body are magnetic poles upon which the mesmerist touching the subject can operate at will. These magnetic poles radiate from the nerve centres where the forces of the physical system concentrate and are thereby made amenable to the will of the operator."

The guide explains, for the comfort of those who may be alarmed, that the mesmeric power is never exercised without the knowledge of the one who wishes to be mesmerised, and goes on to say, after a brilliant description of modes of mental control: "Now clairvoyance is developed in mesmeric states, and the mesmerist often finds upon his hands a subject whom he cannot follow into all the regions that the mind possesses. Though clairvoyance was first discovered through mesmerism, soon the clairvoyant travelled beyond the will of the operator, the body alone remaining subservient to the mesmerist's touch, while the mind investigated remote regions, transcending the thought and going far beyond the will of the lone mesmeriser. This is clairvoyance."

Although mesmerism plays a part, from the Other Side, in the preparation of some mediums for their work, it does not, of course, explain Spiritualism, and Wallace, in making that point clear, sums up the position thus: "The mesmerised patient never has doubts of the reality of what he hears or sees. He is like a dreamer to whom the most incongruous circumstances suggest no idea of incongruity, and he never inquires if what he thinks he sees harmonises with his actual surroundings. He has, moreover, lost his memory of what and where he was a few moments before."

This scientist took all the precautions open to him to prevent or detect fraud in his mesmeric experiments and at the séances in which he took part in private or in public, and his verdict is, "I am quite satisfied that, in the more remarkable manifestations, there is, or can be, very rarely any deception practised." He also draws this distinction between the mesmerised subject who, released from the bounds of the physical body, goes forth into the wider world and brings back reports of what he has seen and heard, and contrasts this with a séance of the kind he attended, say with D.D. Home or Mrs Guppy, another famous medium of that time.

He says of those who attended the séances that they are not in the mesmeric state, "as even our opponents will admit, and as the almost invariable suspicion of fraud, with which the phenomena are at first regarded, clearly demonstrates. They do not lose all memory of immediately preceding events, they criticise, they examine, they take notes, they suggest tests, none of which the mesmerised patient ever does."

He again says, as the result of his experiments in mesmerism and of his experiences at sittings: "The two classes of phenomena [that is, mesmeric and Spiritualist] differ fundamentally, yet there is a connection between them, but in an opposite direction to that suggested." His view was that mediums are sensitives in the mesmeric sense, that they are nearly always subject to mesmeric influence and often exhibit the characteristic phenomena. He found that the most sensitive mesmeric patients were nearly always mediums.

But I must point out that the inquirer should not be led into thinking that it is all due to mesmerism, for mesmerism is merely a means whereby conditions are brought about in which the medium and the guide co-operate for a spiritual purpose that is, to help humanity. Guides work with mediums, and in general direct them, that being a function of a guide, so that the maximum good may be achieved with the minimum of energy. Wallace saw the parallel between his own experiments and séance room phenomena, but—and this is important—he did not confuse the two.

From 1848 to 1862 Wallace travelled in the tropics studying natural history. Now and again he heard of phenomena generally described as table turning and spirit rapping, then common in Europe and America. It was in the early days of Spiritualism, and spirit people were knocking insistently at the doors of this world, clamouring for entrance so that they might be allowed to proclaim the truth of Survival and to encourage men to find a new body of natural laws to explain the phenomena of rapping on and moving tables. Because of his experiences in mesmerism, Wallace hastened home when he heard of the new happenings. For 25 years he had been sceptical of the existence of spirit intelligences until he was compelled to admit them to explain what could not be attributed to natural selection. It did not enter his mind at that time that the marvels of Spiritualism, as he called them, "could be literally true." Like a veritable seeker he says: "If I have now changed my opinion, it is simply by the force of evidence. It is from no dread of annihilation that I have gone into this subject. It is from no inordinate longing for eternal existence that I have come to believe in facts which render this highly probable, if they do not actually prove it. At least three times during my travels, I have had to face death as imminent or probable within a few hours, and what I felt on those occasions was at most a gentle melancholy at the thought of quitting this wonderful and beautiful earth to enter upon a sleep which might know no waking. In a state of ordinary health, I did not feel even this. I knew that the great problem of conscious existence was beyond man's grasp and that this fact alone gave some hope that existence might be independent of the organised body. I came to the inquiry therefore, utterly unbiased by hopes or fears, because I knew that my belief could not affect the reality, and with an ingrained prejudice against even such a word as 'spirit' which I have hardly yet overcome."

Are those noble views the product of an enfeebled mind? Does this come from a deluded man, from one filled with fear or with superstition? Is that the voice of one who is afraid of truth, or one with an ill-informed and badly trained mind? No, there speaks a seeker after knowledge; there speaks the kind of man who is the hope and example of the human race. To him, because of his studies and his knowledge, the earth was beautiful and he was loth to quit it without knowing what lay beyond. His experiences in mesmerism made him the more eager to discover what he could in the spirit knocking and table turning of his day.

His visits to séances began in the summer of 1865, at the house of a friend, a sceptical scientist and lawyer. Only members of his own family were present. They sat at a large, round table, and placed their hands on it. Soon the table began to move slightly. It did not turn or tilt as was common in those days, but with gentle, halting steps went almost across the room. Then slight, distinct tapping sounds were heard. Wallace kept careful records, and the entry for July 22, 1865 reads:

"Sat with my friend, his wife, and two daughters at a large table by daylight. In about half an hour some faint motions were perceived and some faint taps heard. They gradually increased; the taps became very distinct and the table moved considerably, obliging us all to shift our chairs. Then a curious vibratory motion of the table commenced, almost like the shivering of a living animal. I could feel it up to my elbows. These phenomena were variously repeated for two hours. On trying afterwards, we found the table could not be voluntarily moved in the same manner without a great exertion of force, and we could discover no possible way of producing the taps while our hands were upon the table."

Is that a scientific experiment? I think so. It is carefully observed, there is no trickery, the results are unmistakable, the force is clearly not human, as Wallace shows by his tests. At other sittings, after the table had moved and taps were heard, members of the circle would leave the table one by one. But still the phenomena continued, only with diminished strength, until he was left alone with the table, when there were two dull taps or blows, "as with a fist on the pillar or foot of the table, the vibration of which I could feel as well as hear. No one present but myself could have made these, and I certainly did not make them. These experiments clearly indicated that all were concerned in producing the sounds and movements, and that if there was any wilful deception the whole party were engaged in deceiving me."

At another séance, they all sat round a large table for half an hour and nothing happened. Then they sat round a small table. Taps began immediately, and the table moved. Then they returned to the large table and in a few minutes, similar movements and taps occurred. He describes the movement of the table, which made curving motions as if turning on the claws of the leg. Sometimes it would go forward, sometimes backward, sometimes in a zigzag manner across the room. For about a dozen sittings this went on and Wallace concludes:

"Now there can be no doubt that the whole of the movements of the table could have been produced by any of the persons present if not counteracted by the others, but our experiments showed that this could not always be the case, and we have therefore no right to conclude that it was ever the case. The taps, on the other hand, we could not make at all; they were of about the quality that would be produced by a long finger nail tapping underneath the leaf of the table. As all hands were on the table, and my eyes at least always open, I know they were not produced by the hand of anyone present."

In this series of sittings of the home circle, no other phenomena were witnessed. Sometimes they would sit without anything happening, and the scientist concludes that there is no reason why a family of four highly intelligent and well-educated persons should occupy themselves for so many weary hours in carrying out a pointless deception. He sums up these experiments with the comment: "... There is an unknown power developed from the bodies of a number of persons placed in connection by sitting round a table with all their hands upon it."

In the same year he began a series of visits to a public medium, Mrs Marshall, and generally he was accompanied by a friend who was a good chemist, mechanic and a fellow-sceptic. Together they witnessed physical and mental phenomena. A small table, with the hands of four persons upon it, including his own and Mrs Marshall's, rose straight up, a foot from the floor, and remained suspended for about twenty seconds while his sceptical, chemical, mechanical friend sat looking to see if there was anything under the table which supported it in the air.

When sitting at a large table, with a woman on his left and a man on his right, a guitar slid from the woman's hand to the floor, passed over his feet and reached the legs of the man sitting on his right, and then raised itself up slowly until it appeared above the table. Wallace and the man on his right watched this moving guitar carefully all the time. "And it behaved as if alive itself," he wrote, "or rather as if a small invisible child were, by great exertions, moving it and raising it up." All this happened—the table and the guitar incidents—in bright gaslight.

At another séance, a woman sat on a chair, and the chair with the woman on it were lifted. When she left the table to go to the piano, which she had been playing, her chair moved away just as she was going to sit down. When she drew it up again, it moved away. This happened three times. Then it apparently became so fixed to the floor that she could not raise it. A man then took hold of it and found that only by great effort could he lift the chair from the floor. This happened in the light of a bright day, and in a first floor room with two windows. Wallace comments:

"There was no room for any possible trick or deception. In each case, before we began, we turned up the tables and chairs, saw that they were ordinary pieces of furniture, and that there was no connection between them and the floor, and we placed them where we pleased before we sat down. Several of the phenomena occurred entirely under our own hands and were quite disconnected from the medium. They were as much realities as the motion of nails toward the magnet and, it may be added, not in themselves more improbable or more incomprehensible."

CHAPTER THREE

AS EASY AS A B C

WALLACE also investigated mental phenomena, and among his selected experiences are those which go to disprove the claims of sceptics that it all depends on the skill of the medium in hitting the letters which form a name or by the manner in which people dwell on them or hurry over them. These communications were received by the interested person going over a printed alphabet, letter by letter, and when the letters which formed the name were reached, loud taps were heard. In his first communication of this sort, he carefully went over the letters, avoiding any delay or stress. First the raps spelt out correctly the name Para, where his brother died, his christian name, Herbert, and, at Wallace's request, the name of the mutual friend who last saw him—Henry Walter Bates.

At his first sitting with Mrs Marshall, Wallace took a party of five with him. The name of only one member of the party was known to her and this was no clue to the scientist's identity. Immediately, a young woman was told that a message was coming to her. Instead of pointing to the letters of the alphabet one by one, she steadily moved her pencil over the lines. Wallace watched and wrote down the letters indicated by the taps, and the name was the extraordinary one, Thomas Joe Thacker. He thought there must be a mistake, but it turned out that the name was as spelt. It was the name of the young woman's father. Other names were given, as well as places and dates, and all were accurate. But Wallace gives only this one because he made certain that no clue was given whereby it could have been guessed.

Then he took his married sister and her woman friend to another sitting with this same medium, the friend being a stranger. This illustrates how ridiculous is the suggestion that it is all done by guesswork. The unnamed woman wanted the name of a dead relative to be spelt out to her, and with a pointer went through the letters of the alphabet in the usual way while waiting for the psychic tap. Wallace wrote down the first few letters "Y-R-N." The woman who was pointing to the letters of the alphabet said, "Oh, that's nonsense." She wanted to start all over again. There was a tap when she reached the letter "E." Wallace, who realised what was happening, asked for the experiment to go on. The name was spelt out, "YrnehKcocffej." The woman who had asked for the name was puzzled. The name had been split in two—"Yrneh Kcocffej," or plain "Henry Jeffcock," which was the name she wanted.

Included with other experiments with this medium, Mrs Marshall, was this one. A table was examined. A sheaf of notepaper, secretly marked by Wallace, was placed, with a lead pencil, under the centre leg. In a few minutes, taps were heard. Wallace picked up the paper on which was the word William. Another time, he brought from the country a friend who was a stranger to the medium. After a communication which was said to come from the visitor's son, a paper was put under the table and in a few moments, the name "Charley T. Dodd" was found written on it. It was the name of the stranger's son.

Wallace points out that there was no machinery under the table. He asks if it were possible for the medium to slip off her boots, grip the pencil and paper with her toes and write on it a name she would have to guess, then put on her boots again, still having her hands on the table, without any of the sitters knowing what was happening! Wallace tried to see if he could reproduce the phenomena alone. The friend who had accompanied him—the mechanical, sceptical, chemical friend, I presume—had a little psychic power and could produce slight movements of the table. But the communications they received were sufficient to convince them that they were not products of their own mind.

One by one, Wallace went round all his friends to see if he could find a medium among them. He was interested in someone who could produce taps in a clear and distinct manner, because he and his friends, in the conditions which they applied, could not produce them for themselves. Wallace's sister discovered that a woman living with her had this and other forms of mediumship. They sat at a large table without a cloth. All would have their hands on the table and within a few minutes taps would begin. The noises appeared to come from under the table top. The tone and loudness would change from a sound like that produced by a needle or a long fingernail to blows of the fist and slaps of the fingers. There were other sounds like scraping with a fingernail or that of rubbing a damp finger pressed hard on the smooth surface of the table. Wallace was impressed with the speed with which the sounds were produced and changed. Sounds would be made under the table imitating those made by sitters on top of the table. These sounds would keep time to tunes whistled or by themselves would tap out a little tune. He comes to the conclusion: "When these sounds are heard repeatedly in one's own well lighted room, upon one's own table, and with every hand in the room visible, the ordinary explanation given of them seems utterly untenable."

First they thought the taps were made by someone's feet. To test this, all knelt down round the table—but the taps continued, being heard, not only as though coming from the table-top, but they were felt as though vibrating through it. He did not think much of the explanation by scientists of his day that the sounds were made by slipping tendons or cracking joints. If that were so, he says, surely some scientist ought to have been able to bring forward someone whose bones or tendons could make sounds like tapping, rapping, thumping, slapping, scratching and rubbing, and yet repeat these so rapidly as to follow taps of an observer's fingers or keep time to music. The bone cracker or tendon slipper would also have to make the sounds come, not from the body but from a table, and when the tendons slipped or the bones cracked, the table would have to vibrate. No such person has yet been produced.

Wallace continued his experiments. He conducted one to prove that the phenomena were not caused by the current theory which was described as muscular action. The séance party stood round a small worktable, the top of which was twenty inches across. All hands were placed near the centre of the table, which soon rocked from side to side and then appeared to steady itself like a living thing, rose a foot in the air and remained suspended from fifteen to twenty seconds. While this was happening, anyone could strike the table or press it as hard as they pleased, for it resisted considerable force.

The first idea was that someone was lifting the table with his foot. To test that, without telling anyone, he stretched some thin tissue paper between the feet of the table, an inch or two from the bottom of the pillar, in such a way that if anyone placed his foot under it, to try and lift the table, the paper would be crushed and torn. At the sitting, the table rose as before, resisted pressure, sank to the floor, rose again, then dropped suddenly down. Anxiously, and with care, the scientist turned up the table and found the tissue paper intact.

He improved on this test, and made a cylinder of hoops and laths covered with canvas. Inside this the table was placed as though in a well. As it was eighteen inches high, not even the women's skirts could touch the table leg. This contraption did not check the upward movement of the table and all present could watch the medium's hands on the table, certain that nothing could be done under it. Wallace concludes from this: "... it would appear that there is some new and unknown power here at work. These experiments have been many times repeated by me, and I am satisfied of the correctness of my statement of the facts."

Those who have witnessed incidents similar to that reported by the scientist will understand what he describes, when, under favourable conditions he saw "a still more marvellous phenomenon. While sitting at the large table in our usual manner,

I placed a small table about four feet from it, on the side next the medium and my sister. After some time, while we were talking, we heard a slight sound from the table, and looking towards it found that it moved slightly at short intervals, and after a little time it moved suddenly up to the table beside the medium as if it had got gradually within the sphere of a strong, attractive force. Afterwards at our request, it was thrown down on the floor without any person touching it, and it then moved about in a strange and lifelike manner as if seeking some means of getting up again, turning its claws first on one side and then on the other.

"On another occasion, a very large leather armchair, which stood at least four or five feet from the medium, suddenly wheeled up to her after a few slight preliminary movements. It is, of course, easy to say that what I related is impossible. I maintain that it is accurately true, and that no man, whatever be his attainments, has such an exhaustive knowledge of the powers of nature as to justify him in using the word 'impossible' with regard to facts which I and many others have repeatedly witnessed."

This careful and thorough man tells, too, of phenomena witnessed in 1867, when there were present in the circle his sister and five people, while his wife and her sister sat, looking on, some distance from the table. There was no fire in the room and the gas was lowered to give a subdued light, yet one in which everything could be seen. Shortly, they heard taps indicating that the conditions were favourable. A wineglass was placed between a young woman and her father. Soon the glass was tapped gently and a clear, ringing sound was produced, followed by sounds as if two glasses were being clinked gently together. There followed an astonishing demonstration of the number of sounds that could be produced by two glasses, one inside the other, even to the clang of one being dropped inside the other. They were identical with the sounds that could be produced with two glasses manipulated in all ways, yet Wallace was certain there was only one wineglass in the room and that everyone's hands were visible on the table.

Then the glass was put on the table and held by two people to try and prevent vibration, but very soon exquisite delicate sounds were heard, as of a glass being tapped, increasing to the clear, silvery notes of a crystal bell. For some minutes this continued at various degrees of intensity, became gradually fainter and died away. Then a crude harp made of bamboo in the Malay Archipelago, was placed under the table and the strings were twanged as clearly and as loudly as though by human fingers.

Encouraged by the success of the glass, they asked permission to place the bamboo harp on the table to see whether its notes could be imitated by the spirit operators, who agreed to try. In a little while faint vibrating taps were heard which changed into faint twangs forming a distinct imitation of the harp strings but not so successful as the experiment with the wineglass. Then the sitters were told by the spirit guides that the musical sounds were imitated because of the unusual mediumship of a member of the circle. All were so impressed by the accuracy of the psychic imitation of the clinking and tapping of wineglasses, that when the sitting was over the table was turned up under the impression that the spirit people had brought in a second glass unseen. But no second glass was found.

Wallace sums up the experiences which he witnessed in England under test conditions: "It has been objected that we too often use the expression that the phenomena we witness 'could not possibly have been produced by any of the persons present.' I maintain that in this instance they could not, and I shall continue in that conviction until they are produced under similar conditions and the *modus operandi* explained. I have since witnessed a great variety of phenomena both in this country and America ... but I attach most importance to those which I have carefully and repeatedly tested and which give me a solid basis of fact by which to judge of what others relate or of what I have myself seen under less favourable conditions."

What is the standing of Wallace in the scientific world? When, as a young and unknown naturalist, he sent from the tropics his views and theories on natural selection as an integral part of the law of evolution, and his theories on the law of survival of the fittest, he had, while far removed from contact with any other naturalist of his time, arrived at conclusions almost identical with those of Darwin. When Darwin received Wallace's communication he wrote to Lyell: "I never saw a stranger coincidence. If Wallace had my MS sketch written out in June, 1842, he could not have made a better short abstract. Even his terms now stand as heads to my chapters."

It was Lyell and Hooker who advised Darwin to incorporate Wallace's views with his own in the famous lecture which he gave before the Linnean Society. What remarkable process was at work enabling Wallace to arrive at conclusions similar to Darwin while separated from him by 10,000 miles, in an era of slow transport and tardy communication, it is almost impossible to determine. But that he did so is the clearest evidence of an original mind and that he stated his conclusions more briefly than Darwin is a tribute to the quality of his expression. Wallace's work on natural selection ranks with Darwin's origin of species, but Wallace went further than Darwin because he had a wider vision of the natural processes and took into account factors which Darwin did not.

Laymen are apt to consider scientists as an abstract race of men working with a single-minded devotion to impersonal facts, and that they are free from the normal prejudices, inhibitions and plain fears that afflict the ordinary man. This is not so. Here is an example in an estimate of Russel Wallace's contribution to science:

"Whatever may be the future history of his other views [this is obviously a reference to his Spiritualism] he will always be remembered as an originator of a principle more illuminating than any which has appeared since the days of Newton, as one of its two discoverers whose scientific rivalry was only the beginning of a warm and unbroken friendship."

After that you are bound to come to the conclusion that when a work regarded by many as authoritative places Russel Wallace's achievements on a par with those of Newton, he is a man whose testimony on Spiritualism. must be taken seriously. But you have also to record that at the beginning of that tribute there is a hint of prejudice against the scientist's advocacy of Spiritualism, which makes it all the more remarkable that the comparison with Newton was printed. I found the tribute, unsigned, in the 11th edition of the *Encyclopædia Britannica*. It is missing from the 14th edition, which is no compliment to that famous publication, for if, as I believe, the discoverers of the law of evolution have gone far beyond Newton's concept, Wallace cannot be slighted, and Darwin honoured.

Darwin records in his autobiography: "Early in 1856 Lyell [the greatest of all geologists] advised me to write out my views pretty fully, and I began. at once to do so on a scale three or four times as extensive as that which was afterwards followed in my *Origin of Species*; yet it was only an abstract of the material which I had collected, and I got through about half the work on this scale. But my plans were overthrown, for early in the summer of 1858, Mr Wallace, who was then in the Malay Archipelago, sent me an essay *On the Tendency of Varieties to depart indefinitely from the Original Type*; and this essay contained exactly the same theory as mine.

"Mr Wallace expressed the wish that if I thought well of his essay I should send it to Lyell. The circumstances under which I consented, at the request of Lyell and Hooker to allow of an abstract of my MS together with a letter to Asa Gray, dated September 5, 1857, to be published at the same time as Wallace's essay, are given in the *Journal of the Proceedings of the Linnean Society.* I was at first very unwilling to consent, as I thought Mr Wallace might consider my doing so unjustifiable, for I did not then know how generous and noble was his disposition. The extract from my MS and the letter to Asa Gray, had neither been intended for publication, and were badly written. Mr Wallace's essay, on the other hand, was admirably expressed and quite clear."

The joint work attracted little attention, and Darwin came to the conclusion that it was too highly condensed to be appreciated, so he began the long and laborious task of writing out in full his *Origin of Species*. How succinct was Wallace's mind is shown by the fact that Darwin admits that while Wallace explained natural selection easily, he had difficulty in getting even able men to understand it. Darwin says on the success of his book: "Another element ... was its moderate size; and I owe this to the appearance of Mr Wallace's essay; had I published on the scale in which I began to write in 1856, the book would have been four or five times as large as the *'Origin,'* and very few would have had the patience to read it."

Whatever Darwin did in the field of natural selection and the origin of species, equal credit must go to Russel Wallace, and not one word of his work can be belittled because he was a Spiritualist. The same original mind which perceived in the jungles of Borneo the vast concept of an evolutionary law, which reasoned that some of the unexplained phenomena could be attributed only to spiritual agency, must be given credit for seeing in Spiritualism the fulfilment of those views. As a naturalist he conducted experiments, observed their results and was struck forcibly by the existence of a law regulating all life. In mesmerism, as in Spiritualism, he also conducted experiments; equally he observed their results and was struck by another law —the law of the survival of the human soul. Whatever may be the verdict of biographers and the compilers of notices in the encyclopædias, Wallace will be remembered for his service to humanity because he brought to it a proof of which it stood in great need.

CHAPTER FOUR

TESTED IN THE LABORATORY

I WILL try to show, as the story unfolds, that where the human mind enjoys most liberty, there spiritual truth has its greatest success and that where materialistic science flourished in the Western world, where materialism held greatest sway, the minds of scientists and philosophers were released from many superstitions which arose from the theological habits of their time. As a result, men were encouraged to concentrate on the problems before them without considering whether they would upset any of the older ideas. Few succeeded in this grand adventure and as a result less was discovered than was hoped for. Most scientists who considered this question of Spiritualism were convinced before they began that a few experiments would show that it was founded on some psychological freak, or some hitherto undiscovered psychological law, or that it was plain old-fashioned trickery dressed up in a new guise.

It is remarkable that a few raps in a cottage at Hydesville, New York State, should have caused so much perturbation among the leading minds of the age. Yet it was so, and one of the earliest of those who set out to prove that he could explain Spiritualism by natural causes was Professor Robert Hare, of Philadelphia He was an associate of the Smithsonian Institution—founded by a Spiritualist—which is the American equivalent of our Royal Society in this country. Robert Hare, of whom this age knows nothing, was a man of keen intellect, a good experimenter and a sound reasoner. He set to work with a thoroughness equalling Russel Wallace's, and he devised a variety of mechanical devices to ensure that mediums worked under the strictest test conditions.

He satisfied himself that the phenomena were not produced by fraud, sleight of hand, psychological freaks, magnetism, electricity or any of the current theories. The second part of his investigation, to determine whether the intelligence behind the phenomena belonged to people who had once lived on this earth, was conducted under unusual circumstances for a scientist in a most matter-of-fact age; he became a medium. I do not wish to shock sceptical readers too severely at first, but that is a fact and is stated by Dr Hare himself in his book, *Spiritualism Scientifically Demonstrated*, which was published in 1855. He records: "It must be manifest that the greatest difficulty which I had to overcome during the investigation arose from the necessity of making every observation under such circumstances as to show that I was not deceived by the media. But having latterly acquired the powers of a medium in a sufficient degree to interchange ideas with my spirit friends, I am no longer under the necessity of defending media from the charge of falsehood and deception. It is now my own character only that can be in question."

Hare had that sympathetic view of mediums which earned their confidence, and this is important, for mediums are highly sensitive people since their psychic faculties are more developed than those of other people; that is the basis of their mediumship. As a result of this sympathy he was enabled to observe a range of phenomena outstanding in its time. It has to be remembered that his investigations were conducted at the very beginning of Modern Spiritualism, when very little was known factually and when there was a strong tide of antagonistic scientific opinion among those who had not investigated. Many who inquired had mixed results, but Hare had the right mind and psychic nature to achieve success in this difficult period. He did not make the mistake so common in his day of "defying the spirit" to do its best. Nor did he sit down in his laboratory and announce boldly that he would produce results. He realised that the séance room or the home circle can furnish conditions just as scientific as those controlled by instruments of exact measurement and those which register changes in temperature or pressure.

It has also to be remembered that when Hare began his experiments knowledge in physical science was not so great as it is today and that some of the points he argues are now no longer considered, for knowledge has grown. It was a time in which tables in many parts of the world were tilting and tapping, turning and rapping. The great wave of psychic power first rampant in the Rochester knockings swept over the United States and across the Atlantic, touching Britain, France, Germany and Italy. This wave passed over to Russia, causing movements of tables in Moscow and old St. Petersburg. From all records of the time it seems that wooden articles of furniture suddenly became endowed with life, and a Spiritualist wrote: "It appeared that tables had always been made expressly for psychic experiments, that no table was expected to remain at rest on its legs for long, that their true function was not to be seated at or eaten from, but to walk round rooms and spell out messages, to be sat on, stood on, pushed and lifted, all to test whether, by some mysterious power, evidence could be obtained to demonstrate that man survives the grave."

This is not so ridiculous as it would at first appear, for in attempting to break down the walls of materialism which arose naturally owing to the failure of all the world religions at that time, it was necessary for the spirit intelligence directing this missionary work that the attention of men should be called from purely materialistic views to the sensational fact that there was something in the universe which they had not discovered. So knocks were made and tables tilted, scientists were confounded, some were confused, many were irritated and a few, a very few, were irresistibly attracted by the new phenomena. One of the last-named class was Hare who published this letter in the *Philadelphia Inquirer* in July, 1853:

"I am of opinion that it is utterly impossible for six or eight, or any number of persons, seated around a table, to produce an electric current. Moreover, I am confident that if by any adequate means an electrical current were created, however forcible, it could not be productive of table turning. A dry wooden table is almost a non-conductor, but if forming a link necessary to complete a circuit between the sky and earth, it might possibly be shattered by a stroke of lightning; but if the power of all the galvanic apparatus ever made was to be collected in one current, there would be no power to move or otherwise affect such a table." This, it has to be remembered, was written before electric power was as commonly used and understood as it is today, for Davy's first experiments were made only in 1810.

Hare's letter continues: "Frictional electricity, such as produced by electric machines, must first be accumulated and then discharged in order to produce any striking effect. It is in transit that its power is seen and felt." After further observations on the nature of electricity, Hare adds: "I recommend to your attention, and that of others interested in this hallucination, Faraday's observations and experiments, recently published in some of our respectable newspapers. I entirely concur in the conclusions of that distinguished experimental expounder of nature's riddles."

That is how Hare began. He thought it was a hallucination, but he had not then conducted any experiments. He was sure of his ground, he was certain he could explain it all in the terms of material science or he would not have written that assertive letter. The result was an invitation to attend a circle by a Spiritualist, Amasa Holcombe, who wrote of the controversy on table turning:

"I never believed it was caused by electricity or galvanism, but is it not as likely to be by muscular force? You agree with Professor Faraday that the table is moved by the hands that are on it. Now I know, as certainly as I know anything, that it is not true in general, if it is in any instance. There is as much evidence that tables sometimes move without any person near them, as that they sometimes move with hands upon them. I cannot in this case doubt the evidence of my senses. I have seen tables move, and heard tunes beat on them, when no person was within several feet. This fact is proof positive that the force or power is not muscular. If any further evidence was necessary to set aside Professor Faraday's explanation, it is found in abundance in the great variety of other facts taking place through the country, such as musical instruments being played upon without any hands touching them, and a great variety of other heavy articles being moved without any visible cause. If tables never moved except when hands were on them, the case would be different; but as they do move, both with and without hands, it is plain that the true cause remains yet to be discovered."

I quote that letter since it presents Faraday's opinions briefly and shows that the writer, even at that early time, had more experience and more success than Faraday, eminent scientist though he was. Holcombe wound up by saying that if Hare investigated he would find that there was less hallucination and deception than he imagined, his conclusion being: "I have examined this matter for the last three years with as much carefulness as possible, and am not satisfied. If the force is not muscular, as it is certain it is not, I wish science would try again."

Hare admits, at that time, he accepted Faraday's view that it was all due to the muscular action of the hands of the sitters and that there was much hallucination about the subject, though he had not even experimented. He records that even if a spiritual agency had been mentioned as the cause of the phenomena it would have made no impression on his mind at that time, for he says: "Though present on several occasions "when table turning was the subject of discussion, it was not, within my hearing, attributed to spiritual agency. In common with almost all educated persons of the 19th century, I had been brought up deaf to any testimony which claimed assistance from supernatural causes such as ghosts, magic or witchcraft."

Hare went to a home circle, and this is his account of his first séance, momentous because of its consequences: "Seated at a table with half a dozen persons, a hymn was sung with religious zeal and solemnity. Soon afterwards tappings were distinctly heard as if made beneath and against the table, which, from the perfect stillness of every one of the party, could not be attributed to any one among them. Apparently, the sounds were such as could only be made with some hard instrument, or with the ends of fingers aided by the nails."

He found that by means of these tappings questions were answered, the code being one tap for "no," two for "doubtful," and three for "yes," and he records with surprise: "With the greatest apparent sincerity questions were put and answers were recorded, as if all concerned considered them as coming from a rational though invisible agent." Then two mediums sat down at a small table which he carefully inspected and found nothing but bare wood on top and underneath. The drawer of the table was removed, nothing was hidden, and the scientist says: "Yet the taps were heard as before, seemingly against the table. Even assuming the people by whom I was surrounded to be capable of deception and the feat to be due to jugglery, it was still inexplicable. But manifestly I was in a company of worthy people, who were themselves under a deception if these sounds did not proceed from spiritual agency."

He went to another séance at the same house and heard similar tappings on a wooden partition between two rooms. He investigated and found nothing in the rooms which could account for the sounds. Then the medium through whom these manifestations were made held a flute against the panel of the door and asked Hare to listen. He put his ear to the flute and quite clearly heard tapping. As experienced Spiritualists know, there is no special significance in the use of a flute; it was merely a tube used for collecting power. Hare proved that for himself, for the following evening he took with him a sealed glass tube, a hollow glass tube and a brass rod. He held each in turn against the door panel. The rapping was again heard. A long time afterwards he discovered that it was his own father who had rapped on the table at the first sitting he attended, and that it was an old friend who made the sounds in the flute, the glass tubes and the rod. Hare says of the medium, the first with whom he sat, that she would take no money, nor would she allow him to make a present to her child.

His next series of sittings was in another house to which he was accompanied by a critically-minded lawyer who did not believe in Spiritualism. Sounds were again heard, tappings and scrapings, and the lawyer, no matter how he scrutinised the evidence could not find an explanation, nor could he discover a reasonable cause. He also found, as at his first séance, that while he held the small table with all his strength he could not resist its movement when two mediums merely placed their hands on its surface. He discovered, little by little, that messages could be conveyed as easily by tilting a table as by rapping on it or under it. Then he evolved an improved method of communication. He would pass a finger over the letters of the alphabet stuck on pasteboard, and when he came to the required letter the table would tilt or rap. By this slow and laborious method while, as his legal friend observed, the medium had her eyes directed to the ceiling, this message was given: "Light is dawning on the mind of your friend; soon he will speak trumpet-tongued to the scientific world and add a new link to that chain of evidence on which our hope of man's salvation is founded."

Hare's lawyer friend was beaten. He could not understand the means whereby such a message could be composed and translated through the agency of a wooden table. He could not explain how it was known what was going on in Hare's mind. He could not explain why the statements were so positive in their forecast of the scientist's attitude at the end of his experiments, and he was defeated by the prophetic note at the end of the message. Both Hare and the lawyer were left with two explanations—either it was done by sleight of hand or it was produced by some invisible, intelligent being who exercised a mental power and physical force through the table to convey a message. Trickery was dismissed by Hare because of what he observed of the religious and serious character of the circle. He saw how laboriously the messages were obtained and rightly, I think, came to the conclusion that if the Spiritualists with whom he sat were not honest people, they would not have endured their tedious method of obtaining evidence. So he set about devising an instrument which would operate more rapidly than the tilting table, exclude all trickery or possibility of it, and yet demonstrate communication.

Briefly his apparatus consisted of a table, on one leg of which was a wheel that actuated, by means of a pulley, a disc to which letters of the alphabet were nailed. This disc had a pointer, also driven by the pulley, but could not be seen by the medium who sat at the opposite side of the table. To make doubly sure he fixed a zinc screen to the table in front of the medium so that she could not see what was going on. In this primitive piece of apparatus, the pulley was actuated by weights, so that when the table was tilted the disc revolved and, as he found, by spirit agency, was made to stop at the pointer. So, words were formed which made up intelligent messages. Hare was satisfied, and so would any other reasonable person be, that since the medium could not see the letters on the disc, she could not determine which words were being spelt out.

In his first experiment with this method, he said, so that he could be heard in the room: "If there be any spirit present, please to indicate the affirmative by causing the letter y to come under the index." The letter y came under the index. Although the medium could hear Hare's question, it was impossible for her to determine what appeared as a result of the disc's movements, for all she could see was the blank side of the disc as it revolved. The experiment continued with Hare asking the spirit communicator to give his initial. His father's initial then appeared. As a test he asked that the alphabet should be run through in its correct order, the disc stopping at each letter.

Then followed a spelling test. In an interval, members of the circle asked Hare how he could continue in his view that it was all due to hallucination or muscular action through the fingers, when the disc began to revolve and spelt out this message, "Oh, my son, listen to reason." His reply to that was that he must insist on experimental proof that a spirit was present actuating the apparatus. He contended that a matter of such importance could not be held to be proved unless there was further evidence. The medium was at first antagonised by Hare's attitude, and said she would not sit for him again, but later co-operated in further experiments in which he used an improved form of his test table, one which caused the disc to revolve when the table was moved horizontally instead of being tipped.

The results now confirmed the earlier ones. His father communicated and said that his mother and his sister were with him. Hare took this apparatus to another medium, a woman he had not seen before; neither had she seen the table. She sat down behind a screen, and one of the scientist's uncles communicated, spelt out his own name in full, and other names were correctly given. Later he was told by his father that during some of the experiments the spirit communicators found it difficult to spell out the letters of the words they wished to use because they had to focus through Hare's eyes instead of through the medium's. He said that this difficulty was undergone because they wished to give clear evidence that communication by this method could not be explained away by any form of muscular control. Thus it is seen that when the right conditions are provided, spirit people are willing and able to provide, under rigid test, evidence as clear and as satisfying as that obtained in a laboratory for non-spiritual purposes.

The spirits who co-operated with Hare in these test séances were as interested in the success of them as he was. Yet others whom he contacted would have nothing to do with the experiment. One communicator, who was keen that the scientist should succeed in obtaining all the evidence that he sought, said that the test conditions were an added difficulty though the need for them was realised and he suggested a variation in the method. It was that the medium should be allowed to see the revolving disc. It struck Hare at first that this would negative all his precautions, for it was the only means whereby he could be sure that while having her hands on the table she could not influence its movement to produce a word or message on the disc. But he thought of a way out—a flat metal plate resting on some accurately made metal balls which would neutralise any effort made by the medium to cause the table to move. The slightest pressure on the plate would cause the balls to move, so that Hare was certain nothing the medium did could bring about any message she intended to transmit.

He also altered the construction of this table, which he called a "spiritoscope," fitting two legs with castors, and the other two with wheels joined by an axle. One wheel was grooved to carry a band which operated the disc. All this was so contrived that the table had to move nine inches horizontally for the disc to make a complete turn. It was when he reached the stage of this apparatus that he saw the table violently agitated without any observable physical cause being exerted by the medium, whose hands were laid halfway between the centre and the edge nearest to her. Hare records that the table "moved as if it were animated, jumping like a restive horse." It was with this improved test arrangement that he learned how to let the medium see the letters while at the same time making certain that she could not in any way influence the messages appearing on the disc.

The spirit world works in curious ways. When the first attempt was made to use this new table, there were psychic manifestations but no intelligent messages. So Hare tried sitting at an ordinary table with an alphabet card which the medium could not see, and through it was informed that she should be allowed to see the disc with the letters on it. Then, as soon as the medium sat at the bigger table, her hands resting on the plate under which were the balls, the table moved, the disc revolved and messages were spelt out. In the course of a series of sittings the brother and grandfather of the medium manifested, and Hare's father gave the name of an uncle who was killed by Arabs nearly seventy years previously.

Then the table was further improved and extended so that there was not even the slightest possibility of the medium being able to touch the legs. Hare discovered that use of the plate on the balls made it more difficult for the spirits to move the table than when the hands are directly placed on it. His explanation is: "In the latter case the spirits actuate the hands primarily, and the table or apparatus secondarily. But when the hands are incapacitated from influencing the motion, the spirit has to assail the inanimate matter directly, assisted only by an emanation of the medium."

Hare learned, in the course of his investigations, that different classes of spirits are employed for different classes of phenomena and that two grades of beings, one highly spiritual and one less so, were engaged in the experiments to prove that the messages given through the alphabet and the table were not due to muscular action by the medium. As a further variation in his apparatus he evolved a kind of see-saw in which the fulcrum was placed at a point one quarter of the length of the piece of wood. This meant that there was a distance of one foot at one side of the balancing point and three feet at the other. The familiar disc and pulley arrangements were adapted so that they could be actuated by the see-saw which moved when the medium lightly placed her hands at the shorter end of the piece of wood. In this experiment a screen was placed between the eyes of the medium and the disc to make sure that she could not see the letters—and still messages were given.

As a further refinement of his table experiment, instead of asking the medium to place her hands on a plate resting on balls, he introduced a tray on castors. It is thus seen how difficult it would be for a medium to cause a tray on castors to move a table on castors so as to spell out a message on the disc which she wished the scientist to have. Still the evidential messages came and at times the tray on castors would move backwards and forwards rapidly under the medium's hands while the table remained still. Then, at Hare's request, the spirit people would cause the table to move on its castors while the tray on castors remained still. In a further test he asked to be allowed to introduce a metal ball under the tray which should be moved while the ball remained at rest. This, too, was done.

This American scientist was so engrossed in his experiments that he had his test table made in sections to enable him to carry it about from séance to séance in his sittings with strange mediums. Nearly always he obtained evidence. By this means, he obtained the name of his father's business partner, and the name of the business partner of his English grandfather who had died in London many years before. This partner's name was so little known that only Hare was aware of it. Not even his younger brother knew it. Through another strange medium, his father gave the name of an English cousin who had married an admiral and the maiden name of an English relative—Clargess. It was this unusual name which impressed Hare. At another sitting he was allowed to examine the séance room table, about which there was nothing unusual, and found that when the sitters placed their hands upon it, it became repeatedly agitated with an energy which could not be ascribed to the hands placed quietly upon its surface by a circle of persons perfectly quiescent." One of the spirit communicators would, on request, make a sound like a blacksmith hammering, then noises as though she were sawing or sweeping.

The further he went with his experiments, the better the results, all of which went in the direction of proving that his early views on table rapping and tilting being due to hallucinations or muscular movements, were unfounded, for he wrote: "I saw a table continue in motion when every person had withdrawn to about a distance of a foot, so that no one touched it and while thus agitated on our host saying: 'Move the table towards Dr Hare,' it moved towards me and back again." In the same circle he saw a table violently overturned so that its legs were sticking upwards, and while upside down it continued to vibrate when a girl touched it with one finger. While this was happening, the scientist got down on the floor to see what was taking place, and he reported that only the tips of the medium's fingers were touching the table. Hare says that when the table moved without being touched he had a friend watch one side while he closely observed what was happening on the other.

Then he experimented, after seeing tables move without contact, with the upward movement of tables while the medium's hands were gently laid on it. He reported: "On one occasion I saw a large circular table supported by three massive claws of castors overset several times by the influence of three ladies who were media. In order to have this experiment performed with as much precision as circumstances would permit, I seated myself on one side of the table so as to be equidistant from two of the three claws by which it was supported. The intermediate medium was directly opposite the third claw, while the others stood one on each side of her. My relative position was such that, as they were standing upright before me, I could look at their persons partially below as well as above the table. These arrangements having been made, the three media laid their hands on the table a little beyond the margin so that they could not apply their thumbs below the edge and thus assist the table to rise. Under these circumstances, I was enabled to watch the media above as well as below the table by casting my eyes upward and downward alternately, they being all on their feet and standing upright. It was under these conditions, that the table, in three successive trials, came over toward me and went back into its normal position. It did not slam down quickly, when on arriving at such a position as to make it impossible to resist its further descent, but descended gently, rising slowly in recovering its usual upright position."

He continued the experiments, sometimes taking with him to séances people inexperienced but sincere in their desire to know, and by all kinds of tests proved again and again that while spirit operators found it difficult to produce physical phenomena under the stringent test conditions which he imposed, they nevertheless succeeded.

It was at one of these sittings that a friend's dead daughter gave evidence of her identity. When Hare and his friend had talked with her for some time the scientist asked that he might be allowed to conduct an experiment of some scientific importance. He had brought with him an accurately made metal ball and a metal plate ground perfectly flat. He placed the plate on the ball on a table and put the medium's hand on the plate. He knew that any pressure through the medium's hands would be transmitted downward through the legs of the table which would merely be more firmly pressed to the floor. Under these conditions he asked the dead girl if she could cause the table to jerk upward in the same way as it had done during an earlier sitting with her.

The girl's father joined his plea to Hare's, pointing out to his daughter that if this test succeeded it would be strong scientific evidence that the phenomena would achieve through spiritual agency. After a little delay the table rose under the ball, the plate, and the hands of the medium with greater force than when the girl first proved her identity. At a later sitting with another medium, when the girl's father was present with Hare, she communicated again and when asked whether she remembered the test sitting replied through the medium, "You used a plate and ball to support the hands of the medium, which I knocked away."

Hare, through the co-operation of his dead sister, received a good deal of information about spirit methods in causing objects to rise with or without physical contact. Yet it must be borne in mind, when the primitive character of these experiments is noted, that this was the beginning of scientific tests and that we are dealing with a man who, so far, was a sceptic—though he had retreated, or advanced, from the view that it was all caused either by hallucination or muscular movement. Through his sister's assistance he carried out experiments to show that, instead of the table tilting under the medium's hand to cause messages to be spelt out on the alphabet, the table rose. His sister explained that all that happened was that while in one case they operated *through* the hands of the medium to make the table tilt, they operated *against* the hands of the medium to make it rise. Any who have read much Spiritualist literature will understand that there is still no hint of the nature of the force or the method employed from the spirit side to cause all these things to happen.

Another development in these tests was carried out in Hare's own laboratory where he tried a variation of the see-saw. The medium in this case was a boy of eleven. By means of a spring balance Hare found that the downward pressure caused merely by the boy touching the shorter end of the board with a fingertip to be equal to seven pounds. As a further test they got the boy to put his hands in a bowl of water placed at the end—the shorter end—of the see-saw, and again the long end was pulled down, though not so much as when the boy's hands directly touched the board. A witness to the experiment proved that the boy's fingers did not touch the bottom of the bowl holding the water, for he put his hands under the lad's.

A colleague and friend of Hare, Professor Henry, of the Smithsonian Institute, regarded the results as "incredible," and the experiments were repeated with precision and with every precaution. A wire cage was inserted so that it slipped inside the bowl containing water. This cage was supported on either side by a rod so that it was held firm while not touching the sides or coming within an inch and a half of the bottom of the bowl. This is stated to reveal that no amount of physical exertion by the medium could have caused any pressure to be shown at the far end of the see-saw, to which a balance was attached. The water was employed to make it harder for any psychic force to be communicated to the board. The medium clasped his hands and put them into the water until they touched the bottom of the cage. No one else was near the apparatus. Hare silently invoked the aid of his spirit friends, and repeatedly a downward force was exerted equal to 18lbs.

"This experiment has been repeated again and again," he says, "but on a smaller scale, when not only the downward force was exercised but the spelling of words was accomplished." Once, when it was found that the water was too cold and nothing happened, the temperature was raised and results were obtained. Again, with a doctor friend and a medium, all held their hands, touching about a quarter of an inch above a tea-table, and after two minutes it rose in the air and was tossed about from the legs on one side to the legs on the other side with some force. Another time he sat with the Fox sisters in New York after asking each of the six people in the room whether they knew him. None did. Immediately afterwards, his sister communicated and gave her name. He also sat with Mrs Hayden, wife of a well-known journalist of that time. With her he repeated the table tests and obtained messages.

He found, as all other experimenters have found since, that results vary with different mediums, with changes in the weather, in different parts of the country and for other reasons. He sat with mediums who caused the index on his "spirit telegraph" to revolve and spell out evidential messages when their hands were immersed in water, when their hands touched a delicately balanced tray, or when their hands were in the air above the table. He disproved a contention of his time that by putting hands in water the phenomena would cease. He also demonstrated, in experiments with books held open with the back towards the medium and the reading-matter or pictures facing him, that they could tell what was printed on the page or whose picture he was looking at. But curiously he discovered that if the medium had any inkling of what he was looking at, the results were poorer than when they were ignorant of it.

He quotes one experiment which subtly demonstrates this. He held open a book which the medium had not seen before. As usual, the back of the book faced the medium. He looked at a page headed "Publisher's Preface." When the index had spelt out "Publish" it stopped. The medium could not go on. Then she turned to ask her child, who was in the room, to be quiet. The experiment proceeded, and quickly she finished the phrase – "Publisher's Preface." The medium later said she was convinced that the word being spelt out was "publishing," but that her spirit guide, to get that idea out of her mind, distracted her attention by causing her to speak to the child. Then the phrase was completed correctly.

In May, 1858, Dr S.A. Peters carried out a test in Hare's laboratory with a young medium named Ruggles. The medium sat down in front of the spiritoscope and Hare and Peters sat opposite him. Soon the spiritoscope spelled out this message, "Let Dr S.A. Peters put two glass tubes and two pieces of Russian metal in the box." Hare brought Peters two glass tubes about six inches long, half an inch in diameter, hermetically sealed at the ends. He also brought two pieces of Russian platinum rolled into small balls. Peters examined the box into which he was to put the glass tubes and platinum, satisfied himself that all was in order, them locked the box. The two scientists and the medium resumed the sitting. After fifty-five minutes, this message was spelt out on the spiritoscope: "We have a present for Dr S. A. Peters. Let him go to the box and fetch it." Peters did so and found the two pieces of platinum inside the hermetically-sealed tubes. He made this comment: "What I have seen I hold it to be my duty to make known to the world. I have no other interest in making the above statement but the desire to serve my fellowmen."

Hare had tests almost without number in his sittings with the Fox sisters and with others, one striking occasion being when, with a medium who knew not a word of Latin, his father repeated a line from the poet Virgil which he had taught Hare when he was a boy, so years previously. On the same occasion Hare's father reminded him of another word in latin resembling the sound of horses' hooves trampling on the ground, "quadrupedante." Another time through the mediumship of Mrs Gourlay and through his own mediumship, he carried out the following test:

"My spirit sister undertook at one o'clock on the 3rd July, 1855, to convey from the Atlantic Hotel, Cape May Island, a message to Mrs Gourlay, No. 178 North Tenth Street, Philadelphia, requesting that she would induce Dr Gourlay to go to the Philadelphia Bank to ascertain the time when a note would be due, and report to me at half past three. She did report at the appointed time. On my return to Philadelphia, Mrs Gourlay alleged herself to have received a message and that her husband and brother went to the bank in consequence of the idea received by the latter. My sister's report coincided agreeably with his statement to me. All this proves that a spirit must have officiated, as nothing else can explain the transaction."

So, what began with an American scientist declaring publicly in a letter to a newspaper that modern Spiritualism, then manifesting itself in table tilting and table rapping, was an hallucination, ended with scientific conviction and certainty founded upon careful experiments, and with the scientist himself becoming a medium of sufficient power to carry out the test just described in his own words. He had proved not only that table tilting and table rapping were not the result of hallucination or muscular movement but due to the co-operation of spirits and mediums. He demonstrated also that all the phenomena indicated the existence of an intelligent order of beings like his sister who, when he composed a Latin hymn to her through an English-speaking medium, replied in these words:

"I answer your prayer by saying I do watch over you and pray for your welfare. I am grateful for your remembrance and shall strive to deserve it. Our cause is a common one, and we feel the same interest in its promulgation. I am daily striving to disseminate its truths, but can make little progress, having so much ignorance to contend against. I know that the truths of progression, with the help of a good and wise God, will ultimately prevail over all the land; but when that happy time comes to earth, your freed spirit will rove the endless fields of immortality with those loved friends who have gone a little while before. Then will we revel in delights which, in comparison with earth's joys, are far more beautiful and sublime. I wish you could look with the eye of prescience and see that glorious time when all nations shall become as a band of brothers."

That was indeed prophetic in this respect, that Hare has long since gone to join his sister in the spirit world, and the day when mankind shall be as a band of brothers has not yet arrived.

CHAPTER FIVE

"THE IMMORTALITY OF MATTER"

ANOTHER American scientist, Professor Mapes, investigated Spiritualism almost at its birth. His work lay in agricultural chemistry. All his interests were scientific, and he was a materialist. To him, as he watched matter in its processes, there was no place for a deity. He regarded the mind as arising wholly from a human organism and as being actuated by the forces of nature. So, when he came to consider Spiritualism, he speculated, before ascertaining the facts, that it could either be something to do with electricity in an unknown form or else could be explained only by clairvoyance. The atomic theory was not then popular among chemists, who were rather more concerned with force, but he perceived that every element must have an atomic structure, and that in matter there were ultimate atoms which could not be destroyed. That led him to think of the indestructibility of matter or, as he called it, "the immortality of matter."

Step by step, as his investigation of Spiritualism proceeded, over a period of twenty-five years, his views were enlarged until he concluded that from the materialistic viewpoint nature was organised on a one-sided basis—if matter could be proved indestructible and man, apparently the master of matter, did not survive. He took the viewpoint of an investigator. He had no preconceived notions, he did not even begin with Hare's conception and assertion, that it might be explained by hallucination. Nor did he depend upon Faraday's theory of muscular activity. He found, as did Hare, and in much the same way, that objects were moved without human contact, that seemingly inanimate objects became endowed with intelligence.

He proved by experiment that the intelligence was not his nor that of any person present in the room and that the knowledge possessed by these intelligences was either different from or superior to that of all the investigators.

He formed a circle of friends, twelve in all, intellectuals and sceptics, who agreed to hold a weekly circle twenty times to see what would happen. For eighteen of the twenty meetings they sat patiently, and the results were so meagre and so trivial that most of them felt disgusted at what they regarded as a waste of their valuable time. The last two sittings produced phenomena of so striking a character that this circle of sceptics sat for four years, and in the end, or long before it, all became Spiritualists.

"I then discovered," Mapes said, "that persons were made to do things involuntarily. We all know that the system has many involuntary functions, as, for instance, respiration, the circulation of the blood; the action of the brain is also involuntary. But when a violent seizure of the hand takes place, and a communication is given beyond the intelligence of the writer, it is evidence of a wonderful and voluntary action beyond that manifested in the above instances. Little by little I was led to investigate these manifestations, and there came to me a positive revelation in my scientific pursuits. I was then interested in investigating various kinds of soil and their peculiar qualities as adapted to fruit growing. I said, 'If this is true, I may get some idea with reference to the nature of the subject I am investigating.' "

In that he was disappointed, for the guides of the mediums with whom he sat said, "We do not come to aid you in your individual sciences, because we wish to sharpen your own mind to work; but if you will take the first step, we will aid you to take the second." He discovered that chalk and marble were of the same chemical constituencies. He asked the guides whether they would explain to him the difference between the physical construction of marble and chalk which made them different to look at and different to touch, different to handle though chemically the same. The spirit answer was: "Organisation imparts properties different from those that matter previously possessed. Whenever the primitive element in nature passes through an organism it, by virtue of that organisation, becomes advanced."

Then they took him a step further. "Lime," said they, "as found in the bones of animals, is chemically the same as limestone in the soil, but the latter does not fertilise, the former does." So the agricultural chemist created a phosphate of lime and when it was applied to certain soils lacking those elements, nutrition resulted, and he commented: "You may analyse them and you will find that chemistry does not discover why the particle of lime in the human bone is more advanced than a particle of lime in the soil. Here is progression—when one form of atom derives from organisation and advanced function. That function was the point the spirit desired me to understand. Through the combination of atomic elements, a third power is outwrought, and the phosphate of lime never comes back again to the original crude lime we find in the mineral kingdom. Hence all nature is progressive."

He tried to reason out a materialistic explanation which would cover the facts stated by those who believed in Survival, and he had many discussions with his spirit guides. He says frankly that he was such a convinced materialist that he lacked entirely the faculty of intuition. All he did was by the difficult and laborious process of logical reasoning, through which he tried to build up a synthesis that would cover all the facts he knew. He discussed his problems with his wife, who apparently possessed great intuition, for she pointed out the flaws in his reasoning and said that spirit was not a result of any material process on earth but was a principle of life itself.

This frank and painstaking scientist who, while he was on earth, could not grasp the magnitude of the spiritual view of life, nevertheless conceded that his brain could not have evolved the new concepts which came to him after he began his investigation into Spiritualism. So, he reasoned that since there was not a physical cause for his developing views, the source must be spiritual, and in his own way he perceived, little by little, that there was another world as full of unknown elements and powers as ours. But he believed it to be composed of progressed atoms of the kind he had discovered in the evolution of the phosphate of lime from the crude limestone. Though he could not grasp the spiritual view of life he was wholly convinced of the spiritual facts. His daughter was a medium, and through her automatic writing information was given on subjects which she had not studied, and she taught him of spiritual things which he did not verify until he himself passed into the other world.

Another member of his family learned to paint under spirit tuition, and a feature of her mediumship was that no matter what leaf was brought to her, she could paint the whole thing, outline and stalk, as if she knew every feature of the species. Mapes had to confess that this knowledge also came from an outside source. During his investigations he sat with a young man, an unskilled, untaught mechanic who, while under spirit influence, discussed the occult sciences, astronomy, chemistry and geology, and far surpassed the professor in subjects to which he had given many years of study. This convinced the professor that he was communicating not with an ignorant mechanic, but with a highly-informed spiritual being.

64

CHAPTER SIX

PROVING THE FOURTH DIMENSION

OUTSTANDING among the men of science who have by close observation of phenomena proved the reality of psychic powers and the main facts of Spiritualism was Professor Johann C. F. Zöllner, of the chair of physics and astronomy at Leipzig University. When he began his investigation, he was just over forty and was one of the leading men in the Europe of his time. The titles of his books and treatises on learned subjects are not really germane, but they are sufficient to indicate that he was no mere tyro and that he was in fact what I claim him to be, a leading scientist. Associated with him in a remarkable series of sittings were Wilhelm E. Weber, professor of physics, who, with his brother was the founder of the theory of the "vibration of forces," and was an authority on electricity; Professor Scheibner, also of Leipzig University, a mathematician; Professor Gustave Theodore Fechner, a natural philosopher and also professor of physics at Leipzig. Fechner has written a good deal on subjects indicating that his mind was not bound by the material world. For instance, among his works are, *The Soul of Plants*; *The Things of the Future*; *Elements of Psycho-Physics*; *The Problem of The Soul*; and *About The Life Hereafter.*

It may surprise those interested in Spiritualism in the middle of the 20th century to learn that more than sixty years ago[1] the most exhaustive researches were conducted by men of unquestioned standing in their fields which resulted in their publishing conclusions corroborating the claims of Spiritualists and placing many of the assertions on a factual basis. It is almost

1.That is 60 years before this was written in 1945—meaning 1885. (Publisher)

a truism that wherever a noted experimenter has, in co-operation with an outstanding medium, witnessed psychic phenomena, the allegation is always levelled that either the scientist was mistaken or mad, or the medium was a fraud of such refinement and skill that the experimenter was deceived. This charge was made in the case of nearly every outstanding piece of evidence examined in this book, and it follows that there was no shadow of foundation for it.

One of the mediums through whom Zöllner received conviction was Madame d'Esperance (Miss Hope, who later became Mrs Bell). It was she who restored the friendship between Zöllner and Dr Friese, of Breslau University, for though they had nearly everything else in common, they differed over Spiritualism. It was through her that Friese, among the bravest of the brave, announced his conviction of the proof of Survival through mediumship, and so destroyed his own future at the university.

I say this to show that Spiritualism is not an incident or an accident, but is part of a vast plan to touch all minds at all levels. But the medium at whose sittings, mainly in his own home, through whom Zöllner had the most outstanding results, was Dr Henry Slade, an American who was one of the first victims of the ancient Vagrancy Act. He was convicted at Bow Street on a charge of using "subtle crafts and devices by palmistry or otherwise," to deceive Professor E. Ray Lankester, F.R.S., and others. The sentence was three months hard labour, but the conviction was quashed on appeal because of a formal error in the conviction. Zöllner, in his own work *Transcendental Physics*, gives a full account of the proceedings. Lankester had only two sittings with Slade and claimed to have discovered how the spirit writing was done between slates, held together either closely or pressed one above and one below the top of a table.

It is no part of my task to assail Lankester's scientific reputation, but it says little for him that he began his sittings in a spirit of suspicion and with the view clearly in his mind that Slade wrote on the slates when it was held between his legs, or with a piece of pencil stuck in one of his nails. He was naturally pleased when he seized the slates and found that one of them had been written on. Thus, he assumed, fraud was proved.

On the attitude of the Bench towards the mediumship at that time, it is only sufficient to say that the Bow Street magistrate, in spite of the evidence of Russel Wallace and others whose testimony was described from the Bench as "overwhelming", nevertheless excluded it all and decided the issue on the evidence of Lankester and a friend, remarking that his decision was based on "inferences to be drawn from the known course of nature." Such "scientific omniscience" would not be tolerated today if uttered by any magistrate, for, in the light of the knowledge that has been gained since that time, men are less confident in their assertions about the "known course of nature", and how could a magistrate know all the mysteries of nature when in law his decisions are subject to appeal? Into this Bow Street case was imported a professional display by the conjurer, J. N. Maskelyne, whose attempt to show how the séances were conducted was a miserable failure. As in all legal attacks on mediums, the greatest odium arises when the messages which appear, or are relayed, are said to emanate from the dead.

In spite of all this, and in spite of the presumption by the prosecution that Slade "ought to be an impostor" because of the brilliance of his results, none of the scientists on the Continent then interested in psychic phenomena was put off for one second from the intention to sit with him as often as possible. These men were not interested in either religious prejudice or legal ignorance; they desired only to make experiments. Although Lankester continued his persecution in what he called "the interests of science," and objected to Professor Barrett's paper on Spiritualism being read before the British Association, Slade was received generously and kindly in nearly every city he visited, with the exception of Vienna, whence he was deported. To the very end, Slade, in proof of his honesty, offered to give a series of sittings to Lankester to prove the genuineness of his slate-writing, the séances to be held with only the medium and the scientist present, the sole condition to be that if he proved himself genuine, all prosecutions would stop. It is to Lankester's discredit that he did not even answer Slade's letter. So much for the partiality of one scientist, but this highly controversial subject cannot make progress unless the arguments about it are conducted on the widest scale.

The tide of abuse which had welled up in England through the prosecution of Slade, spread to the Continent and was widely printed in German newspapers before the sittings with Zöllner began. Little remains on record of the personality of Zöllner, but throughout all his statements there is a current of generosity that cannot be doubted. He begins his book *Transcendental Physics* with a tribute to Crookes in what would have been most flattering terms if every word he uttered had not been true.

He says of Crookes's researches in Spiritualism, after comparing him with the illustrious pioneers, Faraday and Newton: "Your courage, your admirable acuteness in experiment, and your incomparable perseverance, will raise for you a memorial in the hearts of grateful posterity. ... Accept, then, this work as a token of thanks and sympathy poured out to you from an honest German heart. If ever the ideal of a general peace on this earth shall be realised, this will assuredly be the result not of political speeches and agitations, in which human vanity always demands its tribute, but of the bond of extended knowledge and advancing information, for which we have to thank such heroes of true science as Copernicus, Galileo, Kepler, Newton, Faraday, Wilhelm Weber, and yourself."

So much for the generosity of his nature. Now for his personal courage. "In the first place," he writes, "it is necessary that the truth should be regardlessly outspoken, in order to encounter lies and tyranny, no matter under what shape they threaten to impede human progress, with energy and effect. In this sense I beg you to judge my combat against scientific and moral offences, not only in my own, but also in your country."

It is with those words that Zöllner ended his dedication of the work to Crookes, who had performed in England a parallel service to humanity.

The idea of a fourth dimension is so difficult to comprehend that it is nearly impossible to state it in everyday language. I say this as a preliminary to the fact that Zöllner, who was one of the pioneers of the theory of the fourth dimension, considered that among the results he obtained with Henry Slade was proof of the existence of that dimension. His own views on the subject are prefaced by a summary of the philosophic conclusions of men of the calibre of Kant. Zöllner was convinced that in the series of sittings held in December 1887, in Leipzig, he received proof. Not only that, but he considers also that the séances— all of which were held in the light—supported the views of Newton and Faraday on fundamental questions on which they were at variance with scientists of their times. There is no need for us here to go into these questions. It is sufficient to describe the results obtained by Zöllner, who was so impressed by them that, as a seeker after truth, he could not refrain from showing how the evidence threw light on larger questions which only specialists could discuss with ease.

In some detail this Leipzig physicist claims how a simple experiment of tying knots was shown to prove the existence of a fourth dimension. This arose from the fact that when cords or strips of leather were sealed together at each end, through the mediumship of Slade a series of knots was tied in them. It was deduced from this that the entities responsible for this phenomenon operated outside or beyond the limits of our three dimensions and, therefore, could do what was beyond the powers of those living in a world of three dimensions. Zöllner quotes at some length, in his survey of the scientific and philosophic problems involved in proof of Survival, these words of Immanuel Kant:

"It is, therefore, as good as demonstrated, or it could easily be proved, if we were to enter into it at some length; or, better still, it will be proved in the future—I do not know where and when— that also in this life the human soul stands in an in dissoluble communion with all the immaterial beings of the spiritual world; that it produces effects in them and in exchange receives impressions from them without, however, becoming humanly conscious of them so long as all stands well. It would be a blessing if such a systematic constitution of the spiritual world, as conceived by us, had not merely to be inferred from the—too hypothetical—conception of the spiritual nature generally, but would be inferred, or at least conjectured, as probable from some real and generally acknowledged observation."

Now, all this has taken place. The spiritual world, which is no longer hypothetical but real, has proved its existence in a manner not to be doubted by any man or woman who, with an open mind, earnestly inquires and is content to judge by the facts, and where these are not sufficiently informative in all details, to be guided by reason and the promptings of intuition.

This question of the fourth dimension was held by Zöllner to have been settled experimentally by the simple test of tying knots in endless cords. I do not know whether the imaginative will consider that this experiment is as epoch-making as the alleged incident of the falling apple which, for Newton, was said to be the turning point in his speculations in the theory of gravitation. But the fact is that this German scientist was so impressed by his results with Slade that he had some difficulty in writing with restraint. I think Zöllner is right because his researches have been so uniformly ignored and possibly deliberately neglected. Had his results been obtained purely by means of physical research and by some new device or refinement in apparatus, it is very likely that he would have been hailed as a great pioneer. The prejudice against psychic matters is still so great, though not so great as it was because of the discoveries of men like Zöllner, that much of what we are now examining will receive its due recognition only when a considerable time has passed.

For Zöllner, the problem of the fourth dimension was solved in a few minutes at Leipzig on December 17, 1887, at 11o'clock in the morning, through the mediumship of Henry Slade, of whom a Bow Street magistrate had said that he must have been impostor because the results attributed to him were "outside the known course of nature." Zöllner wrote: "If a single cord has its ends tied together and sealed, an intelligent being having the power voluntarily to produce on this cord four dimensional bendings and movements, must be able, without loosening the seal, to tie one or more knots in this endless cord." In fact, four knots were tied as Zöllner's hands pressed on the cords laid on the table and while Slade's left hand and the hands of another experimenter were all joined.

Zöllner wrote of this test: "While the seal always remained in our sight on the table, the unknotted cord was firmly pressed by my two thumbs against the table surface and the remainder of the cord hung down in my lap. I had desired the tying of only one knot, yet the four knots were formed, after a few minutes, in the cord." The cord was hemp and new, the sealing was done by the scientist the night before the experiment in the presence of several friends and colleagues, while Slade was out of the house. Two other cords of the same quality and dimension were sealed by Weber, the physicist, with his seal the following morning, in his own room.

With all four sealed cords, Zöllner went to the house of a friend where Slade was staying, and the séance began immediately afterwards. This is the precaution taken by Zöllner: "I myself selected one of the four sealed cords, and, in order never to lose sight of it before we sat down at the table, I hung it around my neck—the seal in front always within my sight. During the séance I constantly kept this seal before me on the table. Mr Slade's hands always remained in sight; with the left he often touched his forehead, complaining of painful sensations. The portion of the string hanging down rested on my lap, out of my sight it is true, but Mr Slade's hands always remained visible to me. I particularly noticed that Mr Slade's hands were not withdrawn or changed in position. He himself appeared to be perfectly passive, so that we cannot advance the assertion of his having tied those knots by his conscious will, but only that they, under these detailed circumstances, were formed in his presence without visible contact, and in a room illuminated by bright daylight." Zöllner's colleagues—Fechner, Weber and

Scheibner—-authorised him to say that they were perfectly convinced of the reality of the facts they observed and that there could be no possibility of imposture or sleight of hand.

With that frankness which was his characteristic, Zöllner, in a mood of self-examination, asked himself whether all that happened could have been subjective, and four months after the series of twelve sittings with Slade in which he considered that the reality of the fourth dimension had been demonstrated, he wrote:

"The four knots in the above-mentioned cord, with the seal unbroken, this day still lie before me; I can send this cord to any man for examination; I might send it by turns to all the learned societies of the world so as to convince them that not a subjective phantasma is in question, but an objective and lasting effect produced in the material world, which no human intelligence, with the conceptions of space so far current, is able to explain. If, nevertheless, the foundation of this fact, deduced by me on the ground of an enlarged conception of space, should be denied, only one other kind of explanation would remain, arising from a moral mode of consideration that at present, it is true, is quite customary. This explanation would consist in the presumption that I myself and the honourable men and citizens of Leipzig, in whose presence several cords were sealed, were either impostors or were not in possession of our sound senses to perceive that Mr Slade himself, before the cords were sealed, had tied them in knots. The discussion, however, of such a hypothesis would no longer belong to the dominion of science but would fall under the category of social decency."

Having thus exposed to public gaze all aspects of the case, he pays this tribute to Slade: "Mr Slade produced on me and on my friends the impression of his being a gentleman; the sentence for imposture pronounced against him in London necessarily excited our moral sympathy, for the physical facts observed by us in so astonishing variety in his presence negatived, on every reasonable ground, the supposition that he in one solitary case had taken refuge in woeful imposture. Mr Slade, in our eyes, therefore, was innocently condemned—a victim of his accusers' and his judge's limited knowledge."

At their first meeting, Zöllner asked Slade whether he had ever tried to influence magnetic needles. Questions of this kind were, and still are, of the greatest importance to physicists and electricians. They knew, of course, the laws under which magnetic forces operate on this earth, and were naturally interested to see whether there was either a superior law or a new law of which they had no knowledge. Zöllner was interested in experiments of this nature carried out by von Reichenbach and others. At some length Zöllner quotes this experiment with a medium, the witnesses being Professor Fechner and Professor Erdmann, a chemist, and comments on the influence exercised by a human being on a magnetic needle: "It is so remarkable, and stands so wholly outside our ordinary experience, that it must be a matter of interest to every true investigator of nature to be able to confirm and repeat this fact with another individual." With that in mind, he invited Fechner and Weber to a small gathering of friends who met at his house every week. Slade was invited too, and when it was suggested to him that the assembled scientists would be satisfied with nothing more than the divergence of the magnetic needle under test conditions, he accepted immediately. But Zöllner took the precaution of not telling Slade when the test was to take place. As a preliminary, Slade was asked to move his hand horizontally across the closely-fitted glass cover of a compass fixed in a stand. The needle remained static, and it was deduced from that that Slade had no magnet concealed beneath his skin! This, of course, was written ironically, for the merest tyro who experiments will realise that it is not possible to conceal, without detection, a magnet beneath the skin.

Another attempt was made, and the needle was violently agitated in a way that indicated strong magnetic power. As a result, Zöllner concluded that the tests carried out by his scientific friends with another medium –which I have already mentioned – were confirmed, and he was encouraged to go on. Next evening, with Professors Fechner and Braune, and with Slade, as the medium, they sat at a card table and joined hands on its surface. Immediately raps were heard. Then Zöllner produced a slate which he had bought two hours before and marked it. Immediately spirit writing began on the slate. Zöllner's knife which he had lent to Slade, to cut up a fragment of slate pencil, was laid upon the slate and while the medium was placing the slate partially under the top of the table the knife was suddenly thrown a foot into the air. It landed on the table open; but it had gone up closed! This was repeated several times, and to prove that the knife was not moved in any way by the slate, Slade put a piece of slate pencil on the slate beside the knife and, to fix the position, made a small cross. Immediately afterwards the knife was thrown in the air again and it was seen that the piece of slate pencil remained on the cross on the slate. This was done to prove that by no kind of trickery could Slade have projected the knife into the air by a movement of the slate, for if he had done so the small piece of slate pencil would have moved away from its first position.

Then a double slate was well cleaned, and a piece of pencil placed between them. Slade held the slate over Professor Braune's head, and while he did so scratching was heard on the slate. When it was opened, a lengthy written message was found. While all this was going on, a bed, which stood behind a screen in the room, moved, about two feet from the wall and pushed the screen outwards. At that moment, Slade was four feet from the bed, his back was to it, his legs were crossed, and he was constantly watched by the scientists. The bed was moved back to its original place and the sitting went on. While more experiments were being made with the knife and the slates there was a violent crash. The scientists turned round a little alarmed, and they saw that the screen, which had mysteriously been pushed out by the bed, had fallen apart in two pieces. Strong wooden screws, each half an inch thick, were torn from the top and bottom of the screen—without any visible contact between the medium and the screen. He still had his back to it and the broken parts were now five feet away from him. In a detailed examination of the structure of this heavy wooden screen, to explain that a supernormal force was required to break it, Zöllner, who, it must be remembered, earned his living and gained his reputation by exact observation and accurate experiment, calculates that a force of 198 cwts [1000Kgs] must have been used, roughly equivalent to the power exerted by two strong horses pulling against each other with ropes fastened to the screen, or two teams, each of five men. The scientist also goes into details of the manner in which the force is exerted to prove how abnormal it was, and says:

"We were all astonished at this unexpected and violent manifestation of mechanical force, and asked Slade what it all meant; but he only shrugged his shoulders, saying that such phenomena occurred occasionally, though somewhat rarely, in his presence. As he spoke, he placed, while still standing, a piece of slate pencil on the polished surface of the table, laid over it a slate, purchased and just cleaned by myself, and pressed the five spread fingers of his right hand on the upper surface of the slate, while his left hand rested on the centre of the table. Writing began on the inner surface of the slate, and when Slade turned it up the following sentence was written in English: 'It was not our intention to do harm; forgive what has happened.' We were the more surprised at the production of the writing under these circumstances, for we particularly observed that both Slade's hands remained quite motionless while the writing was going on."

The scientists were so impressed with the results that they decided to ask other scientists to join them—Councillor Thiersch, a surgeon, Herr Wundt, professor of philosophy, and Professor C. Ludwig. Surely no greater number of professors with a variety of training has ever, at one time, attended a séance. They all met at Zöllner's house. On the previous day he had brought a new card table from a local cabinetmaker and put it in place of the table used for previous séances. He left nothing to chance, and was trying to discourage any objection that the older table could have been prepared in some way. Three of these professors, Theirsch, Ludwig and Wundt, sat by themselves for half an hour with Slade, and when they left the room they told Zöllner that the experiment with the pocket-knife was repeated, and that in the test of the double slate, which Slade held in his right hand over the table in full view of all, three sentences were written, in English, French and German, each in different handwriting.

As a further test, Slade sat with Herr Bellachini, the German court conjurer, who gave this testimony: "I hereby declare it to be a rash act to form any conclusion with regard to the objective mediumistic performances of the American, Mr Henry Slade, even with the minutest observation after one sitting only. After I had, at the wish of several highly esteemed gentlemen of rank and position, and also for my own interest, tested the physical mediumship of Mr Slade in a series of sittings by full daylight, as well as in the evening, in his bedroom, I must, for the sake of truth, hereby certify that the phenomenal occurrences with Mr Slade have been thoroughly examined by me with the minutest observation and investigation of his surroundings, including the table, and that I have not in the smallest degree found anything to be produced by means of prestidigitative manifestations, or by mechanical apparatus; and that any explanation of the experiments which took place under the circumstances and conditions then obtaining by any reference to prestidigitation, to be absolutely impossible." This conjurer to the Imperial German Court could at least be considered an expert in sleight of hand, while the professors at Leipzig were unquestionably experts in their several departments of science.

Immediately after this series of tests Slade left to give sittings in Berlin and then at the invitation of the Leipzig scientist returned there. The next series of séances was held at Zöllner's house which, he said, was detached from other dwellings. A card table was paced in the middle of the room and, in addition to Zöllner and Slade, the other sitters were Professors Weber and Schiebner. They all sat with their hands touching. Slade's feet were crossed sideways and he was constantly watched by the scientist sitting next to him. Suddenly, a large handbell which had been placed under the table began to ring and was violently thrown about in full view of all, until it moved horizontally ten feet away on the floor. Immediately afterwards, a small table, fixed to a doorpost by a movable iron support, began to move so violently that a chair standing in front of it was thrown down with a clatter. All these objects were behind Slade, the nearest being five feet from him. While all this was going on, a bookcase filled with many volumes was violently agitated. Then a small thermometer case made of paper was placed on the slate, which Slade held half under the edge of the table. When the slate was withdrawn the thermometer case had disappeared, and it reappeared on the slate after about three minutes. And while this was happening, writing took place continually on the slate!

A second sitting was held not long afterwards for another purpose. Professor Weber placed on the table a compass enclosed in glass. The room was brightly lit with candles. All three scientists linked hands, Slade forming the fourth member of the chain, and as they did so, Slade's hands, both visible, were held a foot away from the compass. After five minutes the needle started to swing violently in arcs from 40 to 60 degrees, and then several times turned through 360 degrees. They tried the experiment of Slade standing at the window, away from the table, but the needle remained stationary, yet when hands were joined again, the needle behaved in the same abnormal manner.

To repeat the experiments carried out by Sir William Crookes and Dr Huggins with D.D. Home, an accordion was placed under the table along with a bell. While Slade clasped the keyless end of the accordion—the keyed end hanging down free away from him—he raised the accordion until his hand, grasping the upper and keyless part, showed above the table. The accordion was held with his right hand. His left hand was placed on the table. Suddenly the accordion began to play and at the same time a bell on a cord rang violently. To make the ringing noise, the bottom of the bell had to be raised from the floor. Then Slade gave the accordion to Professor Schiebner and asked him to hold it as he had done. Hardly had the professor grasped the keyless end of the accordion—as Slade had done a few moments before—when the musical instrument began to play and the bell to dance and ring. All the time Slade's hands were on the table, and his feet, turned sideways, were constantly watched by the other two professors.

Encouraged by their success, Slade then tried an experiment which previously had failed. He handed to Professor Scheibner a slate which Zöllner had bought and kept in readiness. Scheibner was asked to hold it first under the leaf of the table with his left hand, while Slade held it at the edge with his right hand. In this position, Scheibner could tell instantly whether Slade was trying to use the slate. Scheibner's right hand and Slade's left hand were resting on the table. Then the medium said he could feel something damp holding his hand which was grasping the edge of the slate. Hardly had he spoken when Scheibner said he felt a similar thing and that it was like the touch of a piece of damp felt. Scheibner then withdrew the slate, which was found to be quite moist on the upper side, that is, the side that was covered by the extending edge of the table. Both Scheibner's hand and Slade's hand which had held the slate were also moist. While they were all wondering how this moistening was done, and as they were sitting with all hands on the table, suddenly a small, reddish-brown hand appeared at the edge of the table close to Weber, moved rapidly, disappeared and reappeared several times.

Experienced Spiritualists will realise that these sittings were taking place in excellent conditions, otherwise such results could not have been obtained, for already sufficient evidence had been given to satisfy any normal inquirer. But these were not normal inquirers, and a further experiment was begun. Zöllner had suspended a steel ball, about three-quarters of an inch in diameter, by a silk thread inside a cylindrical glass bell a foot high and six inches in diameter. This glass bell was placed under the table and immediately the tinkling sound was heard of the steel ball striking against its sides. Slade's hands were on top of the table, his feet were under observation, and, even if they had not been, the slightest contact of anything with the glass bell would have muffled its sound. Zöllner comments:

"This phenomenon could only be brought about by an elevation of the bell to freedom from contact," that is to say, the glass bell was raised from the floor while the small steel ball suspended by the silken thread struck freely against its sides to produce the tinkling noise. To test this remarkable result, a sitting was held the following day so that the scientists could observe directly what happened under the table. Candles were so placed that the room was well lit. The glass bell was put under the table. Slade sat on the opposite side, his feet, visible to all, being drawn under his chair so that they were about three feet from the glass bell. Shortly afterwards this bell, without any contact by Slade, began to move violently, and rolled about in an oblique position so that the steel ball rubbed itself against the glass side.

At the same sitting, writing occurred on the inner side of one of two slates bound tightly together and laid on a corner of the table, while no physical hand was near them. This striking result was obtained with slates which were bought by Zöllner, cleaned and marked by him. He put a small piece of new slate pencil between the two slates and then bound them tightly together with string. When Weber and Zöllner were busy with magnetic experiments during which all hands were on the table, and while Slade was two feet from the slates, all could hear clearly the sound of writing between the two untouched slates. When separated, this writing was seen: "We feel to bless all those that try to investigate a subject so unpopular as the subject of Spiritualism is at present. But it will not always be so unpopular; it will take its place among the ... (?) of all classes and kinds."

The significance of that question mark is that it was written by Zöllner on the slate before the test was made and Slade had no idea that it was there, and by no conceivable or inconceivable brand of trickery could he have written a message of that kind so that the question mark would take its place in the sentence. If the sentence is read again with the question mark transposed into a word it states: "But it will not always be so unpopular; it will take its place among the questions of all classes and kinds." The question mark is thus seen to have been utilised by the communicating spirit as evidence of intelligence. It is clear from this that the conditions furnished by these scientists were of a different order from the distrust and suspicion in which Lancaster sat with this medium. Nor was this all that happened on this remarkable night, for the large metal handbell was slowly lifted from the floor and without being rung was placed in Zöllner's left hand as he held it close to the table. While this happened Slade's hands were visible to the scientists and his feet were under their control.

Then, as a crowning test, Slade suggested another experiment to prove that he had not tampered with the slates. Picking up the first slate within reach, he laid a piece of slate pencil about the size of a pea on it and held the slate half under the edge of the table so that his hand was under observation. Then he asked Zöllner what he would like to have written on this slate. The answer was: "Littrow, astronomer." Immediately the sound of writing was heard and when Slade drew out the slate, these two words were clearly written upon it, and Zöllner comments: "If Slade did not write the words himself at the time, which from the position of his hand and of the letters upon the slate was impossible (for all the letters were wide apart) so likewise could these words certainly not have been produced by means of a previous preparation of the slate, since the words themselves had occurred to me quite suddenly for the first time."

CHAPTER SEVEN

HE SAW THE "IMPOSSIBLE"

IN the next experiment, a slate was cleaned by Zöllner and was laid open on the floor under the table with a piece of slate pencil on it. Slade then sat with both his hands linked with those of the professors on the table, and his legs were turned sideways so that they were seen all the time. While these precautions were taken, all heard writing being done on the slate under the table. The message on the slate was: "Truth Will Overcome All Error." Then two magnetic needles, one large and the other small, both enclosed in glass cases, were laid on the table in front of the physicist Weber. Hands were joined in the usual way, and while all the experimenters and the medium were at least a foot from the needles suddenly the small needle began to oscillate violently till it was rotating steadily, while the larger needle was so slightly agitated that it might have been caused by shaking the table. None of this movement was caused by the experimenters, who sat still. All were scientists of outstanding reputation and they knew very well that this was one of many critical tests they were making. They realised that they could not have produced such results merely by sitting round a table and holding hands, and they were impressed by the fact that a power new to them was at work.

A moment's analysis will show that the force was intelligently directed, else the one needle could not have revolved while the other was only slightly agitated. An undirected shaking would have caused the same motion in each needle. Yet in the test it was not so, and their satisfaction with what they had already witnessed encouraged these scientists to propose to Slade whether he could cause a non-magnetic steel needle to be magnetised. He said it was doubtful whether that could be done through his mediumship, but after a little while consented to try. Zöllner brought a number of ordinary steel knitting needles, and he and Weber chose one. They proved that it was nonmagnetic by a test with a compass. Slade laid this needle on a slate which he held under the edge of the overhanging part of the leaf of a table—as he did for slate writing—and after about four minutes the knitting needle was again laid on the table. The remarkable result was that only one end of it was magnetised, and so strongly, that iron shavings and sewing needles stuck only to this end, and the needle of the compass was drawn round in a circle easily by it. At the time at which he wrote this account, Zöllner added, "The needle is still in my possession and can at any time be tested." There is no need to dilate on the technical questions involved in this experiment. It happened. It proved that a non-physical intelligence directing a super-physical force did act upon a piece of metal to produce a result, the nature of which was evidential to scientists in circumstances precluding fraud, collusion or mistake.

Several times, while all were holding hands and Slade's feet were in the usual sideways position, the scientists felt the touch of hands under the table and, as we have seen, at least twice a hand was materialised. Now Zöllner decided on a test to gain convincing proof of the existence of those hands, or of the power of the medium and his guides to materialise them. He proposed to Slade that a large, flat porcelain vase should be filled to the brim with flour and placed under the table. Then the medium should ask his guides to put their hands in the flour before touching the scientists. The idea was that the marks of the hands would be clearly visible on the clothing, and at the same time the medium's hands and feet would be under observation. At once Slade agreed. Zöllner filled the vase with flour and they went on with the experiments in magnetism, Slade's hands all the while being visible on the top of the table. Zöllner comments:

"Suddenly I felt my right knee powerfully grasped and pressed by a large hand under the table for about a second, and, at the same moment, as I mentioned this to the others and was about to get up, the bowl of meal was pushed forward from its place under the table about four feet. Upon my trousers I had the impression in meal of a large strong hand, and on the meal surface of the bowl were indented the thumb and forefingers with all the niceties of structure and folds of the skin impressed. An immediate examination of Slade's hands and feet showed not the slightest traces of flour, and the comparison of his own hand with the impression on the meal proved the latter to be considerably larger."

Further experiments were made with magnetising needles, always with the same results, and Zöllner says that Slade "expressed in warm terms his happiness, that he had, for the first time, succeeded in interesting men of sincere inclination to truth for his peculiar endowments, in such a degree that they had resolved to institute scientific experiments with him." Another experiment was tried, of the effect on the medium's sight of looking through prisms. This test is so complicated and difficult to summarise in lay language that all I can say of it is to quote the opinion of these trained observers that they had proved to themselves that changes in his optical powers could be produced. During this test, Slade explained that he was aware of an influence, that is a spirit, who was causing the change in his condition. Phenomena of a more elementary character followed. When Zöllner was talking to the medium, a piece of coal, the size of a man's hand, fell from the ceiling. This was repeated half an hour later in Scheibner's presence. This scientist was talking to Slade and was just on the point of leaving the room when a piece of wood dropped from the ceiling. Another time, while Zöllner was standing near Slade, the scientist's pocket knife was projected through the air and struck Scheibner on the forehead with such force that the scar was visible the next day. Slade could not have thrown the knife because his back was turned to the scientist.

It is natural for a physicist to be more impressed with experiments which leave a permanent record on material objects or in writing than in these sporadic displays of psychic power. To make doubly sure of the assurance which he and others had already received, they decided to try and get an impression of a spirit hand. Zöllner stuck a piece of notepaper on wood and moved the paper over a paraffin lamp without a cylinder until soot was deposited. The wood and paper were placed on the table at which Weber, Zöllner and Slade were sitting for magnetic experiments. While they were thus engrossed, the board with the notepaper on it was. pushed forward with some force under the table and when Zöllner raised it, he found the impression, not of a hand, but of a naked left foot. He immediately asked Slade to stand up and show him both his feet. This was done willingly, the scientists watching while Slade took off his shoes and stockings and they examined these and his feet for particles of soot. None was found. Then he put his foot on a measure, and the difference between that and the impression on the sooty paper was four centimetres. This experiment was repeated two days later, the materials being carefully prepared in the presence of witnesses just before the séance. This time the sooty paper was placed on a broad slate laid under the table around which the séance began. After about four minutes the spirit entities intimated that the slate could be examined. An impression of the same left foot was found on it. Zöllner had this photographed.

This result, because it was so striking, was carefully scrutinised not only by the scientist but by his friend, Herr Thiersch, the professor of criminal law, who had taken a number of impressions for anatomical and surgical purposes, and he compared them with the foot impression produced at the séance. Thiersch's opinion was that the impression obtained in Slade's presence was that of a man's foot tightly compressed by a shoe so that one toe was pressed over the two succeeding toes and only four toe impressions touched the sooted surface. Thiersch explained that the shortness of the foot could have been produced by not putting down the heel and the forepart of the foot at the same time. In proof of all his statements Thiersch produced impressions made on soot. On this Zöllner comments—and it should be clear to the critical reader:

"If upon these observations it should be supposed that Mr Slade had himself produced the impression by putting on his foot in this way, it must first be assumed that he was able to draw off and on his shoes and stockings without application of his hands, which were all along observed by us upon the table; and secondly, that he was so expert in the imposition of his foot on a narrowly limited space that, without seeing the surface he could, nevertheless, always hit upon it with accuracy. This, certainly, would presuppose a large practice in Mr Slade for the object intended, and thereby it must be conjectured that he had been used to bring forward this experiment. Putting aside his lively astonishment and his assurance that such phenomena had never yet been observed in his presence, up to the present time I am not aware of any published accounts of Mr Slade's production of similar facts. That Slade's stockings had not been cut away underneath for this purpose—as was conjectured by some 'men of science' in Leipzig, who in unimportant things accept our physical observations with absolute confidence, but in reference to the foregoing have not hesitated to instruct us in the elementary rules for instituting exact observations—of that as already mentioned, we satisfied ourselves immediately after the experiment."

We have now arrived at the point where Zöllner has been driven into the position in which all genuine seekers after this truth find themselves. He declares that the explanation of the phenomena is as wonderful as the fact, and you can see by his defence of his experiments that he is in the same position as all of us whose word is taken for normal things but is suspected the moment we touch on the unfamiliar, the unorthodox and the "wonderful". Throughout all his record of these outstanding experiments Zöllner constantly returned to his eager desire to prove the existence of a fourth dimension, from which he could infer that intelligent beings dwelt in it and could, with their superior power, produce the results which made such an impression on him. The reasoning which he followed is elaborate and technical and I content myself with an outline of the further experiments which he undertook to prove his theory. He bought two slates, hinged together to form a kind of book. While Slade was absent, he lined the inner surfaces of each slate with paper—his own notepaper. Just before the sitting he spread soot evenly over these two paper surfaces. Then he closed the slates. Afterwards, he said to Slade that if there were such people as "intelligent four-dimensional beings" it would be easy for them to place impressions of feet on the inner surfaces of the closed slate as easily as they had done on sooted paper laid under a table. Slade's response was to be amused. Even his guides, said Zöllner, appeared to be a little taken aback, and in the end made their usual reply, "We will try it." Zöllner sums up this experiment:

"To my great surprise, Slade consented to my laying the closed book slate (which I had never let out of my hands) after I had spread the soot on my lap during the sitting, so that I could continually observe it. We might have sat at the table in the brightly-lighted room for about five minutes, our hands linked with those of Slade in the usual manner above the table, when I suddenly felt on two occasions, the one shortly after the other, the slate pressed down upon my lap, without my having perceived anything in the least visible. Three raps on the table announced that all was completed, and when I opened the slate there was within it on the one side the impression of a right foot, on the other side, that of a left foot, and indeed of the same which we had already obtained on the two former evenings. My readers may judge for themselves how far it is possible for me, after witnessing these facts, to consider Slade either an impostor or a conjurer. Slade's own astonishment at this last result was even greater than my own. Whatever may be thought of the correctness of my theory with regard to the existence of intelligent beings in four-dimensional space, at all events it cannot be said to be useless as a clue to research in the mazes of Spiritualistic phenomena."

Lest it be thought that Zöllner was only a man of science and had no interest in the human aspect of his inquiries, I put it on record that he attacked Virchow, another German scientist, for seeking to impose on Slade test conditions to which the medium objected on the ground that if he succeeded under them there would be still further conditions until his mediumship was lost in a multitude of unnecessary precautions. Zöllner quotes the case of a medium named Eddy, "with every finger of the hand separately fastened by a string nailed to the floor. Eddy's hands are in consequence of these bindings to which they have been subjected for years, quite disfigured. And have all these bindings ever convinced anyone?" Zöllner contended that the simple conditions insisted upon by Slade were sufficient for any experimenter. They were sufficient for him and he, as a physicist and one whose life was spent in research and careful experiment, asserted that the best course was to be as placid as possible and to allow all phenomena to be expressed in conditions in which they could be accurately observed. He also pointed out that Slade never refused to allow anyone to bring his own slates to a sitting, and that anyone armed only with common sense would find sufficient evidence to convince him. Slade, with all his experience of mediumship, insisted that while sitters could bring their own slates he would not have locked boxes or seals, and that as he claimed to be as honest and as earnest as the investigators he must be allowed to have a say in the conditions in which he worked.

As a result of these experiments, Weber, Fechner and others publicly testified to their conviction. In the course of a third series of tests with this medium, Zöllner achieved results as a result of which he publicly risked his reputation of 20 years work as a physicist. With all the sincerity of his nature he says that his description of the phenomena and the results are, in the first place, for physicists. He thought that they, knowing his reputation, would take it for granted that he had observed all the normal precautions of a famous experimenter, and would expect only that the truth should be considered. Still impressed with a desire to continue his experiments on proving a fourth dimension of space he discusses at some length what happened when the knots were tied in endless cords. He says that there must have been a "so-called passage of matter through matter; or, in other words, the molecules of which the cord consists must have been separated in certain places, and then, after the other portion of cord had been passed through, again united in the same position as at first." His view is, that if the fourth dimensional theory is true, the theory of the separation and reunion of molecules would not be necessary. But he reasoned that the fibres of the cord would undergo, during the knotting process, a certain amount of twisting which would be discernible after the knots were tied. He thought about this for some time and then realised that after his original experin1ent he had not submitted the strands of the cord to microscopic examination to determine whether the direction of the fibres had altered in any way. So he undertook this test. He took two bands of soft leather, about 40 inches long, and fastened the ends together and sealed them with his own seal. Then the two bands were laid slightly apart on a table. Slade sat beside him, put his right hand gently over the scientist's hand, which, all the time, was over the leather bands. Slade said he could see lights coming from Zöllner's hands, and Zöllner admitted that all the time he felt a cool wind blowing over them, although he did not see the lights. Then, while the cool wind was still blowing, and Slade's hands were not touching his, he felt the leather bands move under his hands. After hearing three raps on the table, he took his hands away and found that the leather bands were knotted together. The whole experiment took three minutes.

Then Zöllner tried to repeat an experiment carried out with Slade by the Grand Duke Constantine of Russia. It was this. He took a slate and held it with his right hand under the table, while Slade's hands were on the table in front of him. Suddenly a large hand materialised in front of the scientist. It had emerged from under the edge of the table and for two minutes he watched it while the fingers moved quickly. The colour of the hand was pale green, and as he watched it he could see Slade's hands on the table in front of him. While he was still watching, the spirit hand, with a rapid movement, grasped Zöllner powerfully on his left upper arm, and all the time the scientist kept the medium under observation. The spirit hand disappeared and, while Slade's hands were still seen on the table in front of him, Zöllner's right hand was so violently pinched that he could not help crying out. Other incidental phenomena observed by Zöllner, Fechner, Weber and Scheibner were the taking of Weber's gold watch from his waistcoat pocket and then placing it in his hand which he had held under the table. All the time, the medium's hands were under observation. All these phenomena, it must be repeated, took place in well-lighted rooms.

Still with his theory of space well in his mind, Zöllner examined the testimony of other scientists on their results with Slade, and to determine his attitude on his theory, he decided on a test—whether a material body could be made to disappear and reappear in some striking manner. In Zöllner's presence with the scientist named von Hoffmann, Slade asked for a book. This he put on a slate which he held partly under the edge of the table. Soon he withdrew the slate—and the book had gone. The scientists searched the card table, and the small room in which the sitting took place, but the book had vanished. They sat at the table again. Slade was opposite Zöllner, and von Hoffmann between them. Hardly had they sat down when the book fell from the ceiling on to the table, striking Zöllner's right ear violently as it fell. The book appeared to come, says Zöllner, from above and behind him. All the time Slade was seated in front of him and was closely watched. Both his hands were on the table.

At another sitting, in a room brightly lit by the sun, Slade and Zöllner sat down together at a card table. Near them was a round table. Hardly had the sitting begun, with the two men's hands joined, when the round table, some distance away, began to rock slowly and rise until the top of it was above the card table. Then this circular table approached the card table, under which it laid itself with its three feet turned towards Zoller. There was silence for a minute. They were about to ask through the slate what to expect, when the scientist, wishing to take a closer view of the round table as it lay under the card table, looked over and found that the round table had disappeared. They searched the room, but the round table could not be found. Confidently expecting it to reappear they sat again at the card table and waited for about five minutes. Slade then said he could see lights in the air as he followed the direction in which something was apparently moving. All this time, the two men were holding hands and Zöllner could feel the medium's legs touching his own. Slade could not credit that the scientist did not see the psychic lights in the room, but as he turned his head to follow Slade's gaze which was fixed on a point somewhere behind Zöllner's back, the scientist suddenly noticed the table floating at a height of five feet with its legs upwards. They ducked quickly as the round table moved to settle on the card table, but they were not quick enough and Zöllner was struck violently on one side of the head and felt the pain for four hours afterwards.

These results led Zöllner into a further state of reasoning in which he appeared to be convinced that the explanation of the phenomena lay in the existence of four-dimensional beings, although we now know that that is only part of the explanation, and that these beings have the power, in certain conditions, to cause objects to disappear and reappear, as is proved by the large number of apports received since the beginning of Spiritualism. And now we come to what Zöllner himself described as the "miracle experiment." He had two wooden rings turned, one of oak and one of alder. His idea was that if they could be interlinked without being broken it would change scientific conceptions of physical matter and organic processes. He felt that additional testimony would be provided if a biologist trained in microscopy was present at the séance. As further refinements he proposed to see whether the twist markings on snail shells could be altered. For that purpose he bought shells of different species, one common to the neighbourhood and one from the Mediterranean. From a dried bladder he cut an endless band, the point being that if a knot were tied in it microscopic examination would show if it had been broken at any point. He went to a glassblower and got him to blow a ball. Then he cut a paraffin candle to a dimension just small enough to stand up inside the glass ball. Having done so, he asked the glassblower if he could blow a ball round the piece of candle in such a way that the edges would not be melted. The answer was that it could not be done.

Up to this point Zöllner had had thirty sittings with Slade and he was convinced that Slade was but the medium through whom the phenomena occurred and that, therefore, he could not demand that the experiments he had in mind should be guaranteed in advance. His attitude was, he says, the same as that with which he did all his other scientific work, one of passive observation. In the results I am about to describe it has to be emphasised that none of the objects acted upon by the spirit people was touched by Slade at any time during the experiment. Before the sitting began, Zöllner covered the smaller snail shell with the larger so that the smaller one was completely hidden. Then the sitting started. Slade held a slate under the edge of a table in the expectation of some writing. A clattering noise was heard on the slate, and when it was withdrawn the smaller shell was seen. Zöllner concluded that since both shells had lain in the middle of the table when the sitting began he had further proof of the passage of matter through matter. To satisfy himself he grasped the snail shell as it appeared on the slate and it was so hot that he nearly let it fall. He handed it to von Hoffmann, the biologist, who also found it hot.

Some days later, the next part of the experiment was conducted in a brightly-lit room. The two rings of different kinds of wood and the endless band cut from the bladder were strung to a piece of catgut, the end of which Zöllner had tied together and sealed. The scientist and medium sat down at a table, Zöllner placing his hands over the sealed catgut. Near the card table was the round table which on a previous experiment had been made to disappear and reappear. Within a few moments, Slade said he saw lights, and the scientist noticed a smell of burning under the table. Soon afterwards they heard the sound of pieces of wood being knocked together, and when Zöllner asked whether they should close the sitting, the rattling was repeated three times. To their surprise, they found that the two wooden rings, which six minutes before were strung on the catgut, now encircled the leg of the smaller table, and the catgut was tied in two loose knots through which the endless bladder band was hanging undamaged. Zöllner called in his biologist friend and his wife because he was so overjoyed at what he considered his permanent evidence. Then Slade was entranced, and his guide explained that they had tried to carry out Zöllner's wish and tie knots in the endless band of bladder but had to abandon that because of the danger of melting it at the temperature which was generated. The guide said they could see evidence of his statement by a whitish spot on the band, and this was found to be true. After the sitting they tested another piece of bladder by keeping it over a candle and found that a similar white deposit was left.

Zöllner says frankly that the results he expected were not the results he obtained, striking though these were. He had expected the two wooden rings to be interlocked. Instead they were placed round the leg of a table of a different kind of wood. But the seal on the band which had held the rings together was not loosened, the top of the table on which the wooden rings were placed had not at any time been removed and, as far as I know, to the end of Zöllner's life, that table remained intact.

Now this far-seeing scientist, who had sought permanent truth, did not, in fact receive it, for it could be alleged by a later generation of scientists that the top of the table had been removed and the rings inserted over the standard to which the feet were joined. He had received what I call continuing truth—that is to say, a demonstration of a kind that carried scientific research into Spiritualism a stage beyond anything achieved before. There was a case of a similar experiment carried out at the request of Sir Oliver Lodge in which rings of different kinds of wood were interlocked through the mediumship of Margery Crandon, of Boston. At that time it was thought that the mere exhibition of these rings to sceptics, and the recounting of the evidential circumstances in which the materials were prepared and the experiments carried out, would be sufficient to convey truth. It was not so, for after a time the rings were found to have been broken by some unknown agency, and the inference from those long acquainted with tests of this kind is that it is no part of the plan of those in the spirit world who are behind this work to place in the hands of men any tangible evidence which can be described for all time to come, as final proof of the reality of psychic powers, and of the ability of spirit beings in right conditions to prove their superiority over us in the handling of matter and force.

Although he did not suspect it, Zöllner himself had discovered why the experiment took the turn it did. In the course of a discussion with a philosopher who asked him why the spirits who wrote on the slates in Slade's presence did not reveal sublime truths hitherto undiscovered by man, he answered that if that were to happen he would not understand what was being written. Yet, Zöllner did not see that if his experiments had worked out exactly as he had expected, the gulf between him and other scientists of his day who were antagonistic to him and his Spiritualism would have been still wider.

The experiment of obtaining an impression on a sooted paper was repeated by Zöllner's friend, Friese, of Breslau, when the medium, being clairvoyant, described the whole process to the circle of sitters who saw nothing but the results. Dr Nicholas Wagner, a professor of Zoology at St. Petersburg University carried out a similar experiment with a private medium. Included in the circle were an engineer and a chemist. One of the sitters, a woman who began as a professed atheist and materialist became a religious devotee, and when one member of the circle died she promised at a séance that she would materialise. And this she did. At great length, Professor Wagner describes these séances and throughout supports the claims made by Zöllner for the existence of laws, forces and beings beyond the normal, concluding with this declaration: "Again, these facts convince us of the necessity of widening the domain of recognised science and its methods and means for the exploration of the invisible and unknown world, of the existence of which we have in our hearts from childhood so clear, so simple, and so warm a presentiment."

Before he finished his sittings with Slade, Zöllner and his friend von Hoffman carried out an experiment something similar to that in which Dr S. A. Peters and Dr Hare had pieces of platinum transferred to sealed glass tubes. In Zöllner's case coins were removed from sealed boxes after stringent precautions were taken to see that there was no possibility of deception. During these tests Slade gave evidence of clairvoyance, for he read the dates on some of the German coins and gave their value. At the same experiment, two pieces of slate pencil were transferred into a box.

Zöllner was so careful in his experiments that, in the tests to prove the ability of the spirit people to pass matter through matter, he had the assistance of Professor Wach, who taught criminal law at Leipzig University. Wach sealed with his own seal the test slates used in some of the experiments. All these tests are described by Zöllner in detail. Throughout, the spirit guides working through Slade urged on the scientists that the object of their co-operation was to help humanity. In one striking test this message was written on the inside of sealed slates when no one had touched them: "This is a truth not for the select but for all mankind, without respect for rank or race—no matter how one may be insulted or persecuted by his investigations." Experiments were even held to prove that shadows could be cast in such a way as to prove to these scientists that they did not emanate from the objects upon which the light was thrown, or that they were produced in an abnormal manner. Slade sat with many others in Germany and nearly all testified to the remarkable evidence they received in his presence. During one test with slates which he did not touch, and in full daylight, messages were received in English, French, German, Dutch, Greek and Chinese, each with a moral implication and all of them urging those who inquired into Spiritualism in this manner to persevere.

CHAPTER 8

THE MODEL FOR RESEARCHERS

SIR WILLIAM CROOKES carried forward to a remarkable extent much of the work of the scientists who preceded him in the investigation of psychic phenomena. He began with this advantage over many of his contemporaries—that he had neither religious prejudice nor any other kind of bias against facts not commonly accepted. It has been ably argued that irreverence towards all orthodox conceptions and a strictly utilitarian outlook on facts is one of the best attitudes in which to begin a new investigation. This was his attitude at the outset:

"Views or opinions I cannot be said to possess on the subject which I do not pretend to understand. I consider it the duty of scientific men who have learnt exact modes of working to examine phenomena which attract the attention of the public, in order to confirm their genuineness, or to explain, if possible, the delusions of the honest and to expose the tricks of deceivers."

Crookes was the outstanding chemist of his day, his chief work being in the classification and discoveries of the nature of elements. In an estimate of his achievements Sir William A. Tilden, F.R.S., D.Sc., says in his book *Famous Chemists* that Crookes "must be regarded as the chief pioneer in the investigation of phenomena shown in gases under greatly reduced pressure, and his researches must be viewed as the starting point for the discoveries by Sir J. J. Thomson and his school, which have thrown a new light on the constitution of matter." At the age of 16, Crookes began to study at the Royal College of Chemistry, and his first paper based on the result of experimental researches was published in 1851, when he was only 19. This diligent student and experimenter was appointed assistant to his professor, and began researches in photography, a subject which then, technically, was in an almost primitive condition. It would be wearisome even to summarise all the achievements of this remarkable man, but the force of energy that was working in him is shown by the fact that he was not content with being a scientist ut founded a newspaper *Chemical News* in 1859 and remained its editor until 1906. In this journal appeared all kinds of reports on experiments, theories and speculations.

Crookes discovered the metal thallium and announced the fact in his own newspaper. This was the beginning of his recognition as a scientist of international reputation, and in 1863 he was elected a Fellow of the Royal Society. I do not wish it to be understood that I am here suggesting that because that honour was conferred on him that it sets the hall-mark of official science on his discoveries in psychic science. I am merely trying to show that in orthodox subjects he was outstanding, and by all the tests of that school worthy to receive the highest honours it could confer. It is necessary to do this because many who oppose Spiritualism say that the scientists who have declared in its favour are not men of the first rank.

The authorities on the subject say that this discovery by Crookes of thallium involved accurate experiments of a kind guaranteed to test the powers of observation and careful workmanship of any man. In a publication of the American Smithsonian Institute, this appreciation is made of Crookes's work on thallium: "No precaution necessary to ensure purity of material was neglected; the balances were constructed specially for the research; the weights were accurately tested and all their errors ascertained; weighings were made partly in air and partly in vacuum, but all were reduced to an absolute standard, and unusually large quantities of thallium were employed in each experiment ... suffice it to say that the research is a model which other chemists will do well to copy."

Then follows an analysis of a purely technical character which the layman cannot follow and this comment is made upon it:

"This is extraordinary accuracy for so high an atomic weight, at least so far as Crookes's work is concerned." And in his comment on this Sir William Tilden, who wrote Crookes' obituary at the request of the Council for the *Proceedings of the Royal Society* says: "This passage illustrates the spirit which animated Crookes's work throughout. Nothing short of the highest obtainable accuracy ever satisfied him."

Yet it is one of the paradoxes observed in all the history of controversy that it was this very passion for accuracy which was assailed when he courageously published the result of his researches into the phenomena of Spiritualism. One more comment of Tilden's on the outcry which followed the famous chemist's plain statement of observed facts: "It is perhaps not surprising that Crookes was publicly attacked in a violent manner, but he was able to show that many misrepresentations and mis-statements were made which everyone must now perceive were fully unjustifiable. The story of his experiences as told by him is supported by evidence which would be accepted as conclusive if these statements related to any scientific work or to any ordinary occurrence. Crookes himself never withdrew or altered his statements concerning the phenomena he had witnessed, and in his presidential address to the meeting of the British Association at Bristol, so late as 1898, he reiterated his conviction as to their reality. This conviction he retained to the end of his life." Crookes held to his opinions on the truth of Spiritualism for 45 years, and towards the end said that he could add much to what he had already written.

A great deal could be written about his scientific attainments, but we are more directly concerned with his researches into psychic matters. He began his investigations believing that nothing was too wonderful to be true and nothing too small to be overlooked. He laid down for himself this plan of campaign, first to ascertain the facts, then to establish them under test conditions. With his irreverence he began by scoffing at some of the experiments carried out by Spiritualists, and his outlook at that time is summed up in his own words: "The Spiritualist tells of bodies weighing 50 or 100 lbs. being lifted up into the air without the intervention of any known force; but the scientific chemist is accustomed to use a balance which will render sensible a weight so small that it would take ten thousand of them to weigh one grain; he is, therefore, justified in asking that a power, professing to be guided by intelligence, which will toss a heavy body up to the ceiling, shall also cause his delicately poised balance to move under test conditions."

He demanded tests and had to admit that when he talked with leading Spiritualists and outstanding mediums of the day that they were all ready to co-operate with him and were convinced that in the end they would succeed in their claims. Twelve months after he had written his cautious preliminary article in the *Quarterly Journal Of Science* he said this as a result of investigations: "Opportunities having since offered for pursuing the investigation, I have gladly availed myself of them for applying to these phenomena careful scientific testing experiments, and I have thus arrived at certain definite results which I think it right should be published. These experiments appear conclusively to establish the existence of a new force, in some unknown manner connected with the human organisation, which for convenience may be called the Psychic Force." And that was the conclusion after only one year.

Crookes had broken more new ground than he foresaw, for in paying tribute to D.D. Home, the medium with whom most of his results were obtained, he qualifies a little the attitude of scientific iconoclasm which had prefaced his introductory article. He says it was through Home's mediumship "that I am enabled to affirm so conclusively the existence of this Force. The experiments I have tried have been very numerous, but owing to our imperfect knowledge of the conditions which favour or oppose the manifestations of this Force, to the apparently capricious manner in which it is exerted and to the fact that Mr Home himself is subject to unaccountable ebbs and flows of the Force, it has but seldom happened that a result obtained on one occasion could be subsequently affirmed and tested with apparatus specially contrived for the purpose."

Crookes was justifiably sceptical about the alteration in the weights of bodies. All he wanted to see was the moving of a delicately poised balance under test conditions, but after his seances with Home he found: "Among the remarkable phenomena the most striking, as well as the most easily tested with scientific accuracy, are 1 – The alteration in the weight of bodies, and 2 – the playing of tunes upon musical instruments without direct human intervention, under conditions rendering contact or connection with the keys impossible. Not until I had witnessed these facts some half-dozen times and scrutinised them with all the critical acumen I possess, did I become convinced of their objective reality." But he wished to make sure of his certainty, and he invited other scientists to sit with Home in his own house. The sitting was held in a large gaslit room. A drum-shaped cage, made of wooden hoops and narrow laths open at top and bottom, had wound round it 50 yards of insulated copper wire. A net of string was made over the wire, and the apertures were less than two inches long by an inch. The cage was made to slip just under Crookes's dining-table, but too close to the top to permit a hand being pushed in or a foot being inserted underneath it.

A new accordion was bought and Home did not see it or touch it until the séance was under way. Also in the room was an apparatus for testing the alteration in the weight of a body. One end of a strong mahogany board rested firmly on a table while the other end was supported by a spring balance hanging from a sturdy tripod stand. When they were ready to begin the séance, only the weight of the mahogany board, 3lbs., registered on the spring balance. Crookes had called for Home that afternoon and, because they were so interested in their discussion, was with him in his bedroom while he changed his clothes and declared that no secret apparatus was concealed about him. At the séance were Dr Huggins, afterwards Sir William Huggins, President of the Royal Society, a position which Crookes held towards the end of his earthly life, Sergeant Cox, proprietor and editor of the *Law Times* and Recorder of Portsmouth, one of Crookes's brothers, and a chemical assistant.

Home sat in front of the cage which was under the table, Crookes sat close to him on one side, another observer at the other side, and the remaining witnesses at different points in the room to watch what was going on. Most of the evening, especially when striking phenomena were being produced, Crookes and his friend would put their feet on top of the medium's, to test whether he was making any movement. The séance began with Home grasping what I call the blind end of the accordion, that is, the non-musical end, after the bass key, which is at the opposite end, was opened by Crookes, who then drew the cage sufficiently from under the table to allow the accordion to be passed in, keys downwards. Then the cage was pushed as far under the table as possible without catching the medium's arm. Almost immediately the observers on each side of the medium then saw the accordion waving about, it emitted sounds, and finally several notes were played. While this was happening Crookes's assistant got under the table and from that excellent point of observation reported that the accordion was expanding and contracting, but that Home's hand holding the "blind end" was quite still, and the other hand was resting on the table.

Then the accordion began to move about, going round the cage playing as it went. Dr Huggins then looked under the table and declared that Home's hand appeared to be still, even while the accordion was moving and making sounds. Then with his feet controlled by the observers, Home went on holding the accordion, a run of notes was played and a simple air. Crookes's conclusion from that demonstration is: "As such a result could only have been produced by the various keys of the instrument being acted upon in harmonious succession, this was considered by those present to be a crucial experiment. But the sequel was still more striking, for Mr Home then removed his hand altogether from the accordion, taking it quite out of the cage and placed it in the hand of the person next to him. The instrument then continued to play, no person touching it and no hand being near it."

Just for experiment's sake an electric current was passed round the cage, and the accordion, held by Home, again moved about vigorously and was played. The most striking part was yet to come, for the record of this sitting says: "The accordion was now again taken without any visible touch from Mr Home's hand, which he removed from it entirely and placed upon the table, where it was taken by the person next to him, and seen, as now were both his hands, by all present. I [Crookes] and two of the others present saw the accordion distinctly floating about inside the cage with no visible support. This was repeated a second time, after a short interval. Mr Home presently reinserted his hand in the cage and again took hold of the accordion. It then commenced to play, at first chords and runs, and afterwards a well-known sweet and plaintive melody, which it executed perfectly in a very beautiful manner. Whilst this tune was being played, I grasped Mr Home's arm, below the elbow, and gently slid my hand down it until I touched the top of the accordion. He was not moving a muscle. His other hand was on the table, visible to all, and his feet were under the feet of those next to him."

The next experiment was with the board and spring balance. The medium lightly placed the tips of his fingers on the extreme end of the piece of wood which was resting on the firm support, while Huggins and Crookes sat one on either side of him watching for effects. Almost at once the pointer of the balance went down, and in a few seconds rose again. This was repeated several times and the end of the board to which the spring balance was attached was seen moving slowly up and down. Those who do not understand experiments of this kind should realise that it is impossible to cause the spring balance to be moved by ordinary means merely through exerting pressure on the end of the board, which is resting on a firm support which, in turn, is on a table. Direct downward pressure would pass through the board to the support and then down through the table to the floor, and in normal conditions nothing would be registered on the balance but the weight of the board. But, in this case, the fact of the spring balance being moved was proof that a psychic force was at work.

Then the medium took a small handbell and a cardboard matchbox which he saw in the room and placed one under each hand to show that he was not exerting any downward pressure. If he had done so, the cardboard matchbox would have broken, and the handbell would have moved. While his hands were still resting on these two objects, the spring balance oscillated slowly, then became more marked, and Huggins reported that it descended 6½lbs, which, when the weight of the board is subtracted, shows that the pull exerted was 3½ lbs. Examination of the automatic register showed that at one time there was a maximum pull of 6 lbs. To test whether this kind of result could be produced by other means Crookes stepped up to the table and placed his full weight of 140 lbs at the end of the board and jerked vigorously up and down, the net result being that he was about to begin his investigations. When he declared in favour of psychic force and proved by his factual statements that it could be scientifically tested, the normal outcry of the disappointed devotee of the accepted faith and the comfortable convention rose up. All kinds of explanations were advanced to explain away these striking results. Some said that Home was a superior conjurer; others, naively, that Crookes had been hypnotised; yet others said they were too absurd to be treated seriously. The final insult was that he should get better witnesses if he wanted to be believed. It was of little point for this scientist to quote Sir William Thomson in his presidential address to the British Association at Edinburgh in 1871 when he said, "Science is bound by the everlasting law of honour to face fearlessly every problem which can fairly be presented to it." That is all very well when you are addressing the British Association. It is a different matter when you address yourself to the facts of psychic science.

Crookes was disgusted by the opposition of scientists and by the ignorance of newspapers which had previously praised him, but he was not deterred. He advised others who wished to learn the truth about psychic phenomena to experiment as he had done. One objection to his conclusions was that he should have had more tests and with mediums other than Home. He replied that in two years he had found nine or ten mediums with different degrees of psychic power, but he found Home was so powerful a medium and he was so convinced of his genuineness that purely as a matter of convenience he worked with him.

Much has been written about the quality of the results obtained by Crookes, but he had no doubt about what happened, for he declared that he fitted up the apparatus specially for the experiment, and on five separate occasions, objects varying in weight from 25 to 100 lbs. were so influenced by psychic force that he and others with him could hardly lift them from the floor. He wanted to test whether this was a real effect of a hitherto unknown psychic force acting upon matter, or whether it was just imagination.

At the next two sittings with Home, he used a weighing machine when the increase of weight from the 8lbs. rose respectively to 36lbs. 48lbs. and 46lbs. In another experiment with other observers present, weight was increased from the normal 8lbs. of an object to 23lbs. 43lbs. and 27lbs. respectively.

Crookes was in complete charge of the experiments, employed apparatus of great accuracy, excluded every possibility of results being influenced by trickery, and still had all his previous conclusions confirmed. The great Faraday himself did not consider it to be beneath his interest to investigate psychic phenomena, for in a letter to a friend he wrote in 1861 when tests somewhat similar to those carried out by Crookes were proposed: "Is he (Mr Home) willing to investigate as a philosopher, and, as such, to have no concealments, no darkness, to be open in communication, and to aid inquiry all that he can. ... Does he consider the effects natural or supernatural? If they be the glimpses of natural action not yet reduced to law, ought it not to be the duty of everyone who has the least influence in such actions personally to develop them, and to aid others in their development, by the utmost openness and assistance, and by the application of every critical method, either mental or experimental, which the mind of men can devise?"

Crookes's comment on this excellent outline of the conditions which ought to be observed in testing mediums, was, "If circumstances had not prevented Faraday from meeting Mr Home, I have no doubt he would have witnessed phenomena similar to those I am about to describe, and he could not have failed to see that they offered 'glimpses of natural action not yet reduced to law.'" With approval, Crookes refers to the experiment in the alteration of the weight of bodies which Dr Hare carried out in America, the results of which he communicated to the American Association for the Advancement of Science in 1855·

During the period of Crookes's experiments there was great activity in Spiritualist circles, for the famous report of the Dialectical Society was about to be produced giving details of more than 40 experiments supporting Spiritualist claims.

Undeterred by the ill-informed opposition which greeted his results, Crookes did his best to draw the attention of the scientific world to his results, much in the same way that he would have declared a discovery in chemistry or physics. So in June, 1871, he sent a full account of his experiments to the Royal Society, and invited the two secretaries of that body, Professor Sharpey and Professor Stokes, to meet Home at his house and to be prepared for a series of test sittings. The layman, sympathetic to truth and naturally on the side of a defender of that most unpopular cause, might be forgiven a little preliminary rejoicing at the boldness of Crookes's step. The result was as striking as any of the phenomena witnessed in the séance room. Professor Sharpey declined. Professor Stokes replied that he thought there was some defect in Crookes's apparatus, but he condescended thus far: "If I have time when I go to London I will endeavour to call at your house. I don't want to meet anyone, my object being to scrutinise the apparatus, not to witness the effect." Which surely must be one of the most fatuous statements ever made in the long history of science.

The indefatigable Crookes sent a long reply to Stokes in which he explained that he was making an apparatus in which the only contact with the medium would be when his fingers touched water. This apparatus was made in such a way that when the medium's hands were in the water, no mechanical movement could be transmitted to the wooden board to which the spring balance was attached. He explained that he would find a new kind of experiment in which tension was shown in the spring balance when human hands were three inches from it.

He found that Home's power was so great that he could work with large and crude materials and measure the force in pounds. But he proposed a delicate apparatus employing a mirror and a reflected ray of light which would record the changes in weight in fractions of grains.

Crookes was anxious that the Royal Society, having made him a Fellow, should not require him to prove his integrity every time he submitted a statement of facts gathered as the result of psychic experiment. He said if his facts were accepted and his conclusions were rejected by the Royal Society, then he had every right to argue his case before them, but until it could be proved that he was mistaken in his facts, then he would not enter into any discussion until he was proved to be wrong.

Eight days after he had written that he sent another paper on his psychic investigations to the Royal Society. Two days later, Stokes, secretary of that august body, replied, saying that it had not been convenient for him to go to Crookes's house, yet he went on to point out what he regarded as "possible sources of error which occurred to me with reference" to Crookes's first apparatus, "I don't suppose they all exist," he wrote, "but it is evidently, as you yourself would freely admit, for the assertor of a new force to remove all sources of reasonable objection." Then he launched into a technical discussion in which he theorised how the apparatus might have been at fault, and even when he analysed the experiment—in which contact was made through water—he still thought that Crookes's explanation was wrong. As a final blow he said that he did not think much of tremors, "for it would require very elaborate appliances to prove that they were not due to a passing train or omnibus, or to a tremor in the body of one of the company." Then he asked Crookes what he wished to be done with the papers sent to the Royal Society. Crookes returned to the attack by showing that Stokes had altered his opinion from a previous one in which he said that the Royal Society ought not to refuse to admit evidence of the existence of a hitherto unsuspected force. I am going into all this to show how narrow was the margin between the official acceptance by the Royal Society of Crookes's proof of the existence of a psychic force and its rejection by scientists who were biased, if not prejudiced, against the whole subject.

Crookes proved, in a reply based on examination of the experiment and the apparatus with which it was conducted, that the force exerted through the mediumship of Home which moved the spring balance, while his finger-tips rested lightly on the dead end of a wooden board, was equal to 74½lbs. He answered the statement about trains causing tremors by showing that what happened was that the recording apparatus always quivered before the index moved, that the movements were of a slow and deliberate character, taking several seconds for each rise and fall, and that a tremor caused by passing vehicles was a very different thing from a steady vertical pull from 4 to 8lbs. and lasting several seconds.

The answer to Stokes's question—what should be done with the papers?—was that he wished them to be considered although he had no hope that much notice would be taken. He said that many Fellows of the Royal Society were then examining the phenomena under discussion and that it could not be long before scientists all over the world were forced to recognise what was happening. He wanted to be the first in the records of the Royal Society to have made exact experiments, and he regarded it as his duty to keep on sending his results to the society which later, in spite of all prejudice and opposition, made him its President. Crookes was surprised when, a month later, he read a paragraph in *The Spectator* saying that his papers had been rejected because of the "entire want of scientific precision."

The famous scientist pointed out that the papers had not been considered, and he challenged that statement. *The Spectator* replied that the only mistake in its statement was that the opinion of his results had been expressed by a committee. This had not happened; in the absence of a quorum on the committee, Stokes, who most unscientifically had refused to examine the apparatus and to attend the experiment, had decided to issue a statement of his own, as he had power to do. Members of a committee of the British Association then approached Crookes and asked him to do something about it, and a report of sixteen pages was sent to the British Association. Again the inevitable Stokes replied to Crookes after a hasty consideration of the paper, and gave this opinion: "The subject seems to be investigated in a philosophical spirit, and I do not see the explanation of the result of the first class of experiments, while at the same time I am not prepared to give in my adhesion without a thorough sifting by more individuals than one. I don't see much use discussing the things in the sections, crowded as we already are; but if a small number of persons in whom the public would feel confidence choose to volunteer to act as members of a committee for investigating the subject, I don't see any objection to appointing such a committee."

But we have already seen that Crookes found it impossible to gather a representative committee of scientists together for this very purpose. Stokes reveals his prejudice by his final statement: "I have heard too much of the tricks of Spiritualists to make me willing to give my time to such a committee myself." That statement explains nearly everything he did.

CHAPTER NINE

PROFESSORIAL OBJECTIONS DISMISSED

IN self-defence Crookes said it was a pity that a physicist of the eminence of Stokes should have been in such a hurry to decide on the merits of a scientific paper which he could not even have read. He pointed out that Stokes had dropped his previous objection of the "entire want of scientific precision in the evidence adduced" and he had gone as far as to say that "the subject seems to be investigated in a philosophical spirit."

Then Crookes dealt with other professorial objections to his conclusions by men who had not investigated. Representative of these was Professor Allen Thomson who said, at a meeting of the British Association, that no inquiry into psychic force "can deserve the name of study or investigation." One answer to him was a contrary statement by Professor Challis of Cambridge who wrote, "In short, the testimony has been so abundant and consentaneous, that either the facts must be admitted to be such as are reported, or the possibility of certifying facts by human testimony must be given up." Dr Thomson, who could not agree that psychic phenomena were worthy of study or investigation, said that he had been "fully convinced of the fallacies of spiritualistic demonstration by repeated examinations." Yet nowhere in the records of psychic research or psychic investigation is there anything to be found of Thomson's "examinations" as a result of which he made this unsupported declaration: "A few men of acknowledged reputations in some departments of science have surrendered their judgments to these foolish dreams, otherwise appearing to be within the bounds of sanity."

It is one of the commonest accusations against scientists who declare, after investigation, in favour of Spiritualism that their reputations are limited to one field of science and that while they may appear to be sane, there is some doubt about it. No scientist has ever lived who was a master of knowledge over the whole field, and if sanity is to be called into question such a tactic takes discussion beyond the bounds of the controversial and into the criminally libellous for all the distinguished men who declared in favour of Spiritualism, after mature consideration of their own careful experiments, maintained to the end of their days their high scientific reputations and in nearly all cases enhanced them. It is not without significance that the names of nearly all those who violently opposed Spiritualism, and illogically argued against the results of experiments with psychic force, are nearly all forgotten by the general public interested in these matters, while those who declared in its favour and stood by what they had proved to be true are remembered and honoured for their courage.

In Crookes's day discussions on the nature of the atom were becoming a feature at scientific gatherings and he used this as an argument in favour of his claims, saying that what he had proved to be true was verifiable while at the time of which he was writing the theories of the "inner mechanism of the atom", of "interatomic atmospheres" and "gyrating interatomic atoms" were still theories. What he had discovered was of practical and immediate use, while the speculations of that day into the nature of the atom were—just speculations. You would have thought that in a materialistic age the discovery by an outstanding chemist of a new force would have revolutionised thought, but it did not. What the explanation may be, it can hardly be dealt with here, yet the fact remains that since that day scientific inquiry has gone a long way round until now, physicists, who are still largely concerned with atomic problems, in their speculations and inevitable theories are slowly coming to take a non-materialistic view.

Crookes had not embarked on a wide and sweeping campaign of generalities. He was stating facts, all of which were simply and experimentally verifiable. That the secretaries of the Royal Society of that day did not choose to witness investigation is a censure on them and this action on their part may have contributed largely to the neglect of the study to which Crookes and others had opened the way. But this consolation remains, that whatever the scientists may have neglected, either deliberately or because of preoccupation with other matters, it is true that a vast fund of knowledge has passed into the possession of the common people, many of whom have developed their own psychic gifts and proved in their own homes that phenomena of a nature similar to those observed by Crookes and others can be produced in the right circumstances. It was a happy coincidence that the brave declarations of Crookes coincided almost with the beginning of compulsory education, and enabled millions who otherwise would have remained in the dark to learn of a great truth. Whether it was intentional or accidental would be difficult to prove, but the fact remains.

How far astray a protagonist may go is illustrated by the declaration of Professor Huxley, quoted by Crookes in the midst of this controversy, for Huxley observed: "If there is one thing clear about the progress of modem science, it is the tendency to reduce all scientific problems, except those that are purely mathematical, to problems in molecular physics—that is to say, to attractions, repulsions, motions and co-ordination of the ultimate particles of matter! Yet these ultimate particles, molecules or atoms are creatures of the imagination, and as pure assumptions as the spirits of the Spiritualist."

In preparation for this book I read a volume entitled *Atoms in Action* by an American, Professor George Russell Harrison, in which progress is recorded in the employment of atoms for the use of man and a good deal of it, especially in photography, is due to the work of Crookes with the infra-red ray. There is no need to weary the reader with long technical descriptions, but to prove how mistaken Huxley was, as a convinced materialist, in his attack on those interested in atoms, Harrison gives a description of an iconoscope, the "eye" of a television transmitter.

Television has been observed by millions of people, and its existence can no longer be doubted by anyone of reasonable education—not even by an anti-Spiritualist. The description of the "eye" of a television transmitter is: "By means of a camera lens, an image of the scene to be broadcast is formed on a square screen. This image is then scanned with a beam of high-speed electrons shot from the electron gun in the tube .... The resulting vibrations in the current which leaves the screen are then amplified thousands of times before being broadcast." Huxley, whatever his other qualities, had not the gift of foresight, let alone that of prophecy, and his gibes at atoms, molecules, particles, spirits, and Spiritualism are all proved by the facts to be worthless and untrue.

Crookes's comment on the attitude of mind of Huxley and those who thought with him is: "Men thought before the syllogism was invented, and, strange as it may seem to some minds, force existed before its demonstration in mathematical formulae." And, if I may be allowed to point out, it went on existing afterwards. Another objection made to Crookes's conclusions was that Home was a "man possessed of a great power which he called 'electro-biological', by which he cast an influence over all those present." Crookes had not heard of this strange power and replied that whatever may have happened to himself and those who witnessed the experiments, the recording instruments were certainly not hypnotised. At this late date it is useless to regret that other scientists did not accept the open invitation which Crookes extended to them.

To demonstrate the intensely practical nature of his work he showed by fact and by illustration that the effects of Home's psychic power could be registered by an apparatus operated by clockwork, and movements upwards and downwards of the spring balance were recorded on a sheet of glass by a steel point. In these experiments, decrease of gravitation as well as an increase was recorded, but since Crookes was especially interested in the increase of weight he dealt most with that phenomenon. He tried over and over again the effect of psychic power on the spring balance with which there was no direct contact, the medium's hand being placed in a bowl of water suspended from a stand which at no point touched the board to which the spring balance was attached. He found, in time, that it made no difference to the general effect of the psychic force whether the medium's hands rested on the dead end of the board or whether they were placed in a bowl of water. So, the glass vessel and the iron stand were removed and Home's hands were made to touch the stand holding the board and spring balance. But it must be emphasised that this was at the end removed from the spring balance, for the slightest pressure at the live end, to which the recording machine was attached, would produce results.

To test whether there was any muscular control a witness put his hand on Home's hand and placed one foot on both of Home's feet, and Crookes watched both all the time. Then the clockwork mechanism which allowed the recording steel point to pass over the glass screen was set in motion and a curve was drawn showing the rise and fall of the psychic power. In some of these tests, and in earlier ones, minute as well as gross differences were recorded. In a further test Home was asked to stand one foot from the wooden board, and another tracing was made on the glass showing the action of the psychic force. On yet another occasion, while the medium was three feet from the apparatus and his hands and feet were tightly held, there was a demonstration of the power of the medium to cause the instrument to move in an easily recorded manner.

With another medium a further trial was made with a delicate apparatus which was tested beforehand and no efforts at jumping or shaking the apparatus or its stand, or by stamping on the floor, caused the lever to be influenced. The woman medium then stood at the side of the apparatus nearest the dead end of the board and was asked to put her finger on the wooden stand. Crookes placed his hand over hers to detect whether there was any muscular movement, and presently percussive noises were heard on a parchment in the recording apparatus. It was like the dropping of grains of sand. A fragment of graphite, which the scientist had placed on a membrane, was projected slightly into the air and the recording end of the lever moved slightly up and down. Sometimes the sounds were like the sparking of electricity, and at other times there was an interval of a second or two between each sound. The same apparatus was used with D.D. Home, the only difference being that there were few sounds and the lever moved more slowly. The result of these meticulously careful experiments led Crookes to this conclusion:

"These experiments confirm beyond doubt the conclusions at which I arrived in my former paper, namely, the existence of a force associated, in some manner not yet explained, with the human organisation, by which force increased weight is capable of being imparted to solid bodies without physical contact. In the case of Mr Home, the development of this force varies enormously, not only from week to week, but from hour to hour; on some occasions the force is inappreciable by my tests for an hour or more, and then suddenly reappears in great strength. It is capable of acting at a distance from Mr Home (not infrequently as far as two or three feet), but is always strongest close to him. Being firmly convinced that there could be no manifestation of one form of force without the corresponding expenditure of some other form of force, I for a long time searched in vain for evidence of any force or power being used up in the production of these results. Now, however, having seen more of Mr Home, I think I perceive what it is that this psychic force uses up for its development.

"In employing the terms vital force, or nervous energy, I am aware that I am employing words which convey very different significations to many investigators; but after witnessing the painful state of nervous and bodily frustration in which some of these experiments have left Mr Home—after seeing him lying in an almost fainting condition on the floor, pale and speechless— I could scarcely doubt that the evolution of psychic force is accompanied by a corresponding drain on vital force. To witness exhibitions of this force it is not necessary to have access to known psychics. The force is probably possessed by all human beings, although the individuals endowed with an extraordinary amount of it are doubtless few. Within the last twelve months I have met in private families five or six persons possessing a sufficiently vigorous development to make me feel confident that similar results might be produced through their means to those here recorded, provided the experimentalist worked with more delicate apparatus, capable of indicating a fraction of a grain instead of recording pounds and ounces only."

All this serious, scientific work is not without a humorous side. A leading mechanical engineer in the United States, Coleman Sellers, published a whole criticism of Crookes's experiments, a point of which was that he doubted whether the mahogany board used in some tests weighed only six pounds. Crookes's reply was that he tested this fact on four separate balances in his house, and then he got the greengrocer to weigh it. The mahogany board still weighed only six pounds.

Crookes was not left in peace. His conclusions were assailed in the *Quarterly Review* by a physiologist whom I suspect to be Dr Carpenter, who had lectured him in private at a meeting in Edinburgh of the British Association. This physiologist would not allow any interruptions, refused to permit Crookes to express his point of view, let alone state his conclusions, and for an hour harangued the great chemist. The upshot of all his tirade was that Crookes was said to be mistaken—that all the phenomena were due to "unconscious cerebration" and to "unconscious muscular action."

It was in vain to point out to this garrulous man that, in the experiments on which Crookes had based his scientific paper for acceptance by the Royal Society, the medium had not even touched the apparatus. He went even further than criticism. He asserted that Crookes was compromising the Royal Society and declared that he ought not to be allowed to send papers on the subject to that august body. The reason why Crookes spent no time at all in refuting statements about "unconscious cerebration" or "involuntary muscular action" is that he did not observe either of them; he was concerned only with what he saw. The attacks were prejudiced, full of misstatements, and even went to the length of asserting that Crookes had no scientific reputation, until this scientist was forced in his own defence to publish the facts and to speak of his own achievements in a way that must have been distasteful to him. He said that, apart from experimental work on psychic phenomena, he had probably read more works on the subject and on subjects related to it, in English, French and Latin than any other man in the country.

To the accusation that he was unacquainted with Faraday's instrument for testing table turning, Crookes replied with an account of his meeting with the great experimenter. Crookes was friendly with the manager of a firm of scientific instrument makers and says: "I was in his shop several times a week ... and I had many conversations on the subject of table turning. I well remember his telling me one day that Professor Faraday had given him the design of a test apparatus by which he expected to prove that the rotation of the table was due to unconscious muscular action. A day or two after, he showed me the instrument which he was just about to send to Professor Faraday. At that time, I was not infrequently favoured by the late Rev. J. Barlow, secretary of the Royal Institution, with invitations to his house in Berkeley Street, and on one of these occasions, on entering the room he thus accosted me: 'Mr Crookes, I am glad you have come, we are doing a little table turning, and have just been trying Faraday's new instrument. He is here, let me introduce you to him.'

"Professor Faraday, in his kindly genial manner explained to me fully the action of his instrument, and instead of poohpoohing the remarks of a mere boy—for I was only 21—listened to my objection that his instrument was based upon the assumption that the supposed acting force from the hands would pass through the glass rollers, and replied that he thought of that and had got over the difficulty by tying the two boards together so as to render them rigid, when it was found that the table rotated as well with the instrument as without it. Since then I have frequently employed the device of a long delicate indicator to magnify minute movements. I have adopted it from 1853 up to the present time. In my early experiments I availed myself of Professor Faraday's test instrument, but recently when I have frequently made it a *sine qua non* that the operator shall not touch the table or any portion of the instrument, it would puzzle even the ingenuity of my reviewer to say how Faraday's instrument is to be applied. In such cases, I adopt a well-known and superlatively delicate index, a ray of light."

Now Faraday is often quoted by anti-Spiritualists as the scientist who exposed it all, but this factual account of the meeting between Crookes and Faraday, and of the subsequent experiments proving the existence of a psychic force should, for all time, dispense with the need of the materialist to rely on such an unwarranted statement.

It was even suggested that Crookes was not entitled to be a Fellow of the Royal Society, and that the honour was conferred with "considerable hesitation." Crookes was obliged to state the facts, which were that he was invited to allow his name to go forward. When he was admitted it was stated at the meeting of the council, "There is on the part of the chemists now on the council a sincere appreciation of your high claim." And the friend who wrote that to him congratulated him on being one of the fifteen elected. Crookes says that there were probably fifty candidates and each one was carefully scrutinised. He was thirty-one when he became F.R.S., an unusual distinction for such a young man. He pointed out, too, that the applications of some candidates were postponed from year to year, some even for ten years. That answered the allegation that there was "some hesitation" about his election. It was alleged, too, that he was only a specialist. His answer was to ask a series of questions in which he stated his own achievements:

"Is it general chemistry, whose chronicler I have been since the commencement of *Chemical News* in 1859. Is it thallium, about which the public have probably heard as much as they care for? Is it chemical analysis, in which my recently published *Select*

Methods is the result of twelve years work? Is it disinfection and the prevention and cure of cattle plague, my published report on which may be said to have popularised carbolic acid? Is it photography, on the theory and practice of which my papers have been very numerous? Is it the metallurgy of gold and silver, in which my discovery of the value of sodium in the amalgamation process is now largely used in Australia, California, and South America? Is it in physical optics, in which department I have space only to refer to papers on some phenomena of polarised light which I published before I was twenty-one; to my detailed description of the spectroscope and labours with this instrument, when it was almost unknown in England; to my papers on the solar and terrestrial spectra; to my examination of the optical phenomena of opals, and the construction of the spectrum microscope; to my papers on the measurement of the luminous intensity of light; and my description of my polarisation photometer? Or is my speciality astronomy and meteorology, inasmuch as I was for twelve months at the Radcliffe Observatory, Oxford, where, in addition to my principal employment of arranging the meteorological department, I divided my leisure time between Homer and mathematics at Magdalen Hall, planet hunting and transit taking with Mr Pogson, now Principal of the Madras Observatory, and celestial photography with the magnificent heliometer attached to the observatory? My photographs of the moon, taken in 1855, at Mr Hartnup's observatory at Liverpool, were for years the best extant, and I was honoured by a money grant from the Royal Society to carry out further work in connection with them. These facts, together with my trip to Oran last year, as one of the Government Eclipse Expedition, and the invitation recently received to visit Ceylon for the same purpose, would almost seem to show that astronomy was my speciality. In truth, few scientific men are less open to the charge of being 'a specialist of specialists'."

There were further attacks and further replies, but the brave inquirer went on until he arrived at a point in his experiments where he declares: "The phenomena I am prepared to attest are so extraordinary and so directly opposed to the most firmly-rooted articles of scientific belief—amongst others, the ubiquity and invariable action of the force of gravitation-that even now, on recalling the details of what I witnessed, there is an antagonism in my mind between reason, which pronounces it to be scientifically impossible, and the consciousness that my senses, both of touch and sight—and these corroborated by the senses of all who were present—are not lying witnesses when they testify against my preconception." To support this line of argument he quotes a letter from a scientific friend of high standing in which it is said: "I see that it is not reason which convinces a man, unless a fact is repeated so frequently that the impression becomes like a habit of mind, an old acquaintance, a thing known so long that it cannot be doubted. This is a curious phase of man's mind, and it is remarkably strong in scientific men stronger than in others, I think. For this reason we must not always call a man dishonest because he does not yield to evidence for a long time. The old wall of belief must be broken by much battering."

In a passage full of candour as the result of critical self-examination, Crookes goes on to his own viewpoint in which he says that it is folly for critics to assume that people who are sane and rational in other matters suddenly lose their reason because they investigate facts which are well attested. He tells his own story of how this difficult and extensive subject came to be studied by him. He intended to give only his leisure time to it. He found there was something in it and was determined, as a student of natural laws, to follow wherever the facts might lead. The inquiry of a few months became the work of years, and if he could have afforded it I do not doubt he would have given a very long time to the experiments. All that held him up then was the lack of sufficiently powerful mediums who could work with him. He, who had begun by truly scientific scepticism about the views expressed by Spiritualists, at this stage of his inquiry admitted that to the very earnest Spiritualism was a religion and the mediums in family circles were jealously guarded instruments. Sometimes, he records, that as a personal favour he was allowed to attend a home circle.

One other medium he sat with was Kate Fox (Mrs Jencken) one of the famous Fox sisters through whom modern Spiritualism was founded. He discovered, in the course of many séances, that contrary to that section of public opinion which was wholly antagonistic to things psychic, all séances did not have to take place in darkness. Except where darkness was essential to the production of certain phenomena, of luminous appearances and a few other cases, everything that he discussed took place in the light. He answered in advance the allegation that he could have been deceived by conjurers. Even if the most skilful illusionist had all his elaborate machinery and showed his tricks in a place and at a time at his own choosing, they could not, says Crookes, have equalled what he saw: "I need only say that, with very few exceptions, the many hundreds of facts I am prepared to attest ... have all taken place in my own house, at times appointed by myself, and under circumstances which absolutely precluded the employment of the very simplest instrumental aids." He says further that he chose his own circle of friends for séances, introduced the firmest sceptic he wished, and imposed his own test conditions. He experimented with the effect of various kinds of light and found that the interfering rays on psychic matters appeared to be those at the extreme ends of the spectrum.

Then he classified the phenomenon of the movement of heavy bodies with contact by the medium but without mechanical exertion. He proved many times that the medium did not pull, push or lift the objects; nevertheless they moved. You will recall that at the outset of his researches he was anxious to see whether a difference of weight in grains could be recorded in this class of phenomena. After a few years he came to the conclusion that this phenomenon was of itself of little importance, and he was more impressed by the attendant occurrences—a peculiar cold air, "sometimes amounting to a decided wind. I have had sheets of paper blown about by it, and a thermometer lowered several degrees. On some occasions ... the cold has been so intense that I could only compare it to that felt when the hand has been within a few inches of frozen mercury."

Under the heading of the "phenomena of percussive and other allied sounds," he classified "delicate ticks, a cascade of sharp sounds, detonations in the air, sharp metallic taps, a cracking like that heard where a frictional machine is at work, sounds like scratching, the twittering of a bird." Each medium with whom he sat he found produced special phenomena, those with Home being the most varied and those with Kate Fox the most powerful. With Miss Fox he found that she had only to put her hand on anything and bangs would be heard within it like a triple pulsation. Sometimes this would be loud enough to be heard several rooms away. He recorded these sounds inside a living tree, on a sheet of glass, on a stretched iron wire, on a stretched membrane, on a tambourine, on the roof of a cab and on the floor of a theatre. It was not always necessary for Kate Fox to touch the object from which the sounds were emitted. They occurred on floors and walls when her hands and feet were being held, when she was suspended in a swing from the ceiling, when she was enclosed in a wire cage, and when she had fallen fainting on a sofa. He heard the noises on his own shoulder and under his hand, on a sheet of paper held between his fingers with a piece of thread passed through one corner of the paper. He tested every alternative theory to account for the production of these sounds, but could not escape from the conviction that they were "true objective occurrences not produced by trickery or mechanical means."

Early in his inquiry he was confronted with a question, "Are the movements and sounds governed by intelligences?" Not long afterwards he discovered that the movements were not caused by blind force but that in the phenomena there was something "associated with or governed by intelligence."

Sometimes he found the intelligence was below that of the medium, sometimes in opposition to the medium and sometimes of a character that led to the belief that the intelligence "did not emanate from any person present." He was satisfied that all the demands he had made at the outset of his inquiry on the alteration of the weights of bodies had been fully met. "Those are the phenomena of the third class," he writes, "and in the fourth class are the movements of heavy substances at a distance from the medium." Some of his experiences in this class are:

"My own chair has been twisted partly round, whilst my feet were off the floor. A chair was seen by all present to move slowly up to the table from a far corner when all were watching it; on another occasion an armchair moved to where we were sitting, and then moved slowly back again, this at a distance of about three feet at my request. On three successive evenings a small table moved slowly across the room, under conditions which I had specially prearranged, so as to answer any objection which might be raised to the evidence." Several times the experiment was repeated in which a heavy table was moved in full light, the chairs turned with their backs to the table, about a foot off, and each person kneeling on his chair with hands resting over the backs of the chair, but not touching the table. On one occasion this took place when he was moving about so as to see how everyone was placed.

Five times a heavy dining-table was raised between a few inches and eighteen inches off the floor, when precautions had been taken to make trickery impossible. Once a heavy table rose from the floor in full light while he was holding the medium's hands and feet. Yet another time the table was raised from the floor when no one was touching it, again under test conditions, arranged by Crookes.

In the sixth class of phenomena recorded by him was the levitation of human beings. This occurred four times in the darkness under test conditions which satisfied him, but he described only those cases in which he saw all that happened. Once he saw a chair with a woman sitting on it rise several inches from the ground. At a later test, to answer any charge that it might have been a trick, the medium knelt on the chair in such a way that all its four legs were visible. The chair then rose about three inches, remained suspended in the air for about ten seconds, and slowly descended to the floor. In full daylight two children were raised from the floor with their chairs while he was kneeling to keep a close watch on what happened. Three times he saw Home raised completely from the floor, once when he was sitting in an easy chair, once when he was kneeling on a chair, and another time when he was standing up.

Then he attested to the most striking account of all, the instance in which Home was levitated and carried through the window at a point So feet above the street and then returned into the room. Three of the witnesses, the Earl of Dunraven, Lord Lindsay, and Capt. C. Wynne, gave him first-hand accounts of what took place and he comments: "To reject the recorded evidence on this subject is to reject all human testimony whatever; for no fact in sacred or profane history is supported by a stronger array of proofs. The accumulated testimony establishing Mr Home's levitations is overwhelming."

In class seven, is the movement of various small articles without contact by anyone, including the playing of an accordion in his own hand while he held it, keys downward. Then the accordion flew about the room, playing all the time; window curtains were waved; some force pulled up venetian blinds eight feet from the sitters; tied a knot in a handkerchief and threw it in a far corner of the room; played notes on a distant piano; caused a card plate to float about the room; raised a water bottle and tumbler from the table; made a coral necklace rise on end; caused a fan to move about and fan the company; and set in motion a pendulum enclosed in a glass case which was firmly cemented to the wall.

In class eight, were luminous appearances, such as points of light darting about the room, the answers to questions by flashing a bright light in front of his face, sparks of light rising from the table to the ceiling and falling on it with an audible sound, alphabetical communication—by flashes occurring before him in the air—a luminous cloud floating upwards to a picture while under the strictest test conditions. Several times he had a solid, self-luminous, crystalline body placed in his hand by a hand which did not belong to any person in the room.

"In the light," he says, "I have seen a luminous cloud hover over a heliotrope on a side table, break a sprig off and carry the sprig to a lady; and on some occasions, I have seen a similar luminous cloud visibly condensed to the form of a hand and carry small objects about." Still in the light, he saw phenomena, classified as class nine, in which he saw hands. "A beautifully formed small hand," he says, "rose up from an opening in a dining-table and gave me a flower; it appeared and then disappeared three times at intervals, affording me ample opportunity of satisfying myself that it was as real in appearance as my own. This occurred in the light in my own room, whilst I was holding the medium's hands and feet."

He saw a thumb and finger pick petals from a flower in Home's buttonhole and lay them in front of people sitting near them; he saw a hand playing the keys of an accordion while both the medium's hands were visible and held by people near him. All the hands and fingers he saw were human, lifelike and graceful. Sometimes they were icy cold and at others as warm and firm as those of an old friend. He tried sometimes to prevent these hands from escaping from his grasp. Without a struggle the hands gradually lost shape, dissolved into vapour and almost melted from his clasp.

In class ten was direct writing in conditions prearranged by himself. "I have had words and messages," he testifies, "repeatedly written on privately marked paper, under the most rigid test conditions and have heard the pencil moving over the paper in the dark." In class eleven were phantom forms and faces, and this was what led him to one of the greatest séances in all Spiritualism. But before we go into that, consider his description of the spirit forms he saw. At his own home when Home was standing about eight feet from the curtains of a window, "a dark, shadowy, semi-transparent form, like that of a man, was seen by all present standing near the window, waving the curtain with his hand. As we looked, the form faded away and the curtains seemed to move." Then he gave a more striking instance, still with Home: "A phantom form came from a corner of the room, took an accordion in its hand, and then glided about the room playing the instrument. The form was visible to all present for many minutes, Mr Home also being seen at the same time."

In class twelve he began to consider the question of exterior intelligence. At a sitting with D.D. Home, an intelligence, asked to give a message in morse, which code Crookes thought no one else in the room but himself knew, tapped on his hand with a wooden lath, and gave him the message he had asked for. He was convinced that a good morse operator was manipulating the piece of wood. To test whether some automatic writing which a medium was doing was due to "unconscious cerebration", he asked, "Can you see the contents of this room?"

"Yes," was the answer. "Can you see this newspaper?" said Crookes, who without turning round to see what he was doing, put his finger at random on a copy of the "Times." "Yes," was the reply, through the planchette. Then the scientist asked that the word which his finger covered should be written.

Slowly the planchette wrote the word "however". Crookes turned round and saw that the tip of his finger was covering the word "however". He had purposely avoided looking at the newspaper before making the test, and recorded that it was impossible for the medium to have seen the word. He says that Home, with whom he sat frequently, was often searched before and after the sittings.

CHAPTER TEN

MEDIUM TRIUMPHS IN CRUCIAL TESTS

AND now for the materialisation which occurred through the mediumship of Florence Cook. Round her there raged the usual controversy centred in all outstanding materialisation mediums. For, in this case, the evidence was so striking, indeed, the evidence was so solid, as to become the materialisation in fact of the hopes and dreams of those who yearn for irrefutable proof of survival after death. Crookes reduced all the arguments to this, that when the spirit guide, Katie King, was visible in the room, the body of Florence Cook, the medium, was to be in the cabinet. Proof, he said, should be absolute and not inferred by reason or because seals remained sealed, knots remained knotted and stitches remained intact. He had the best reason to know that in this class of phenomena locks, which are no proof against love, cannot prevent the manifestation from appearing to confirm what others have seen, and further to confound the confused and sceptical. Florence Cook was as shabbily and as cruelly treated by anti-Spiritualists as any materialisation medium who has since followed her.

At one séance the usual preliminaries were gone through, the room was searched and the medium then entered a "cabinet" formed by drawing a curtain across a small room which adjoined a larger room. Soon afterwards, Crookes records, the form of Katie "appeared at the side of the curtain, but soon retreated, saying her medium was not well and could not be put into a sufficiently deep sleep to make it safe for her to be left. I was sitting within a few feet of the curtain close behind which Miss Cook was sitting and I could frequently hear her moan and sob, as if in pain. This uneasiness continued at intervals nearly the whole duration of the séance, and once, when the form of Katie was standing before me in the room, I distinctly heard a sobbing, moaning sound, identical with that which Miss Cook had been making at intervals the whole time of the séance, come from behind the curtain where the young lady was supposed to be sitting. I admit that the figure was startlingly lifelike and real, and, as far as I could see in the somewhat dim light, the features resembled those of Miss Cook; but still the positive evidence of one of my own senses that the moan came from Miss Cook in the cabinet, whilst the figure was outside, is too strong to be upset by a mere inference to the contrary, however well supported."

This was in answer to allegations when attacks were made on the medium and Crookes followed his testimony. He said that the medium was giving him an exclusive series of private séances in which it was promised by Katie King that he would be allowed to make any test he chose. Some months later, he wrote, "I am happy to say that I have at last obtained the 'absolute proof' to which I referred." To light up the séance room without harming the medium, Crookes devised a phosphorus lamp, merely some phosphorised oil in a tightly corked bottle.

At one séance the materialised form of Katie walked among the experimenters for some time, retreated behind the curtain which had been drawn across the laboratory to form a cabinet, emerged in a minute, called Crookes over and said to him: "Come into the room and lift my medium's head up. She has slipped down." Katie was standing before him in her white ectoplasmic robe and turban headdress. Crookes went into the library behind the laboratory, Katie stepping aside for him to pass, and he found Miss Cook had slipped from the sofa and her head was in an awkward position. He lifted her back to the sofa and in doing so had satisfactory evidence, in spite of the darkness, that the medium was not attired in the same costume as Katie, but was still wearing her ordinary black velvet dress, while the materialised spirit was clad in white robes of ectoplasm. There could not have been any quick change, because it took him only three seconds to lift the medium up to the sofa.

He went back to join the others. Katie reappeared and said she would like to be able to show herself and the medium at the same time. Katie asked for the phosphorus lamp, as the gas had been turned out, and after showing herself in the glow of Crookes's ingenious device, she handed the lamp back to him and said, "Now come in and see my medium." He followed her into the library and by the light of his lamp saw the medium on the sofa just as he had left her. He looked for Katie, but she had gone. He called her, and there was no answer. Crookes went back to his place, and Katie reappeared and told him she had been standing close to the medium all the time. Then she asked if she could try an experiment, took the phosphorus lamp and went behind the curtain, but she came back in a few minutes, handed back the lamp and said there was not enough power to do what she wished. Crookes's son, a boy of fourteen, told his father that from where he was sitting he could see behind the curtain and he saw the phosphorus lamp floating about over Miss Cook, illuminating her as she lay motionless on the sofa, but he could not see anyone holding the lamp. Of a séance held not long afterwards, Crookes says: "Katie never appeared to greater perfection, and for nearly two hours we walked about the room conversing familiarly with those present. On several occasions she took my arm when walking, and the impression conveyed to my mind that it was a living woman by my side, instead of a visitor from the other world, was so strong that the temptation to repeat a recent celebrated experiment became almost irresistible. Feeling, however, that if I had not a spirit, I had at all events a lady close to me, I asked her permission to clasp her in my arms, so as to be able to verify the interesting observations which a bold experimentalist has recently somewhat verbosely recorded. Permission was graciously given, and I accordingly gave—well, as any gentleman would do under the circumstances." Of course he kissed her; the famous scientist kissed a materialised spirit!

Now Katie said she would try the experiment of showing herself and her medium at the same time. Crookes took his phosphorus lamp into the room which was being used as a cabinet, asking a friend who was skilful at shorthand to make a note of anything that was said. And with these notes before him he writes: "I went cautiously into the room, it being dark, and felt about for Miss Cook. I found her crouching on the floor. Kneeling down, I let the air enter the lamp, and by its light I saw the young lady dressed in black velvet, as she had been in the early part of the evening, and to all appearance, perfectly senseless; she did not move when I took her hand and held the light quite close to her face, but continued quietly breathing. Raising the lamp I looked around and saw Katie standing close behind Miss Cook. She was robed in flowing white drapery as we had seen her previously during the séance.

"Holding one of Miss Cook's hands in mine, and still kneeling, I passed the lamp up and down so as to illuminate Katie's whole figure and satisfy myself thoroughly that I was really looking at the veritable Katie whom I had clasped in my arms a few minutes before, and not at the phantasm of a disordered brain. She did not speak but moved her head and smiled in recognition. Three separate times did I carefully examine Miss Cook crouching before me, to be sure the hand I held was that of a living woman, and three separate times did I turn the lamp to Katie and examine her with steadfast scrutiny until I had no doubt whatever of her objective reality. At last Miss Cook moved slightly, and Katie instantly motioned me to go away. I went to another part of the cabinet and then ceased to see Katie but did not leave the room till Miss Cook woke up and two of the visitors came in with a light."

Then he gave the points of difference which he observed between the medium and the spirit as she materialised: "Katie's height varies: in my house I have seen her six inches taller than Miss Cook. Last night, with bare feet and not tiptoeing she was four and a half inches taller than Miss Cook. Katie's neck was bare last night; the skin was perfectly smooth both to touch and sight, whilst on Miss Cook's neck is a large blister, which under similar circumstances is distinctly visible and rough to the touch. Katie's ears are unpierced, whilst Miss Cook habitually wears earrings. Katie's complexion is very fair, while that of Miss Cook is very dark. Katie's fingers are much longer than Miss Cook's, and her face is also larger. In manners and ways of expression there are also many decided differences."

It is inevitable that in a work of this character much has to be quoted from the works of scientists who did the original researches, which are here being summarised. Without any apology, I again quote from what I regard as a classic séance in a religion which has tens of thousands of absolutely evidential events to prove its claims. This is the story of the departure of Katie King whose work with the medium, Florrie Cook, had come to an end. Non-Spiritualists do not realise—and there is no reason why they should—that there grows up between the medium and the guide, and those who are associated with them in a common task, a bond of friendship based on co-operation which after some time becomes affection and, in most cases, a deep and unselfish love. I do not say that that was the relationship between Crookes and Katie King, for there is no evidence of it, but it certainly was the bond between Katie King and Florence Cook, her medium.

"During the week before Katie took her departure," writes Crookes, "she gave séances at my house almost nightly to enable me to photograph her by artificial light. Five complete sets of photographic apparatus were accordingly fitted up for the purpose, consisting of five cameras, one of the whole-plate size, one half-plate, one quarter-plate, and two binocular stereoscopic cameras, which were all brought to bear upon Katie at the same time on each occasion on which she stood for her portrait. My library was used as a dark cabinet. Those of our friends who were present were seated in the laboratory facing the curtains, and the cameras were placed a little behind them, all ready to photograph Katie when she came outside, and to photograph anything also inside the cabinet, whenever the curtain was withdrawn for the purpose.

"Each evening there were three or four exposures of plates in the five cameras, giving at least fifteen separate pictures at each séance; some of these were spoilt in the developing, and some in regulating the amount of light. Altogether I have forty-four negatives, some inferior, some indifferent, and some excellent. Katie instructed all the sitters but myself to keep their seats and to keep conditions, but for some time past she has given me permission to do what I like, to touch her and to enter and leave the cabinet almost whenever I please. I have frequently followed her into the cabinet and have sometimes seen her and her medium together, but most generally I have found nobody but the entranced medium lying on the floor, Katie and her white robes having instantaneously disappeared."

What check did Crookes have on the conduct of the medium in the intervals between the séances? Just this: "During the last six months Miss Cook has been a frequent visitor at my house, remaining sometimes a week at a time. She brings nothing with her but a little handbag, not locked; during the day she is constantly in the presence of Mrs Crookes, myself, or some other member of my family. There is absolutely no opportunity for any preparation, even of a less elaborate character than would be required for enacting Katie King. I prepare and arrange my library myself as the dark cabinet, and usually, after Miss Cook has been dining and conversing with us, and scarcely out of our sight for a minute, she walks direct into the cabinet, and I, at her request, lock its second door and keep possession of the key all through the séance; the gas is then turned out, and Miss Cook is left in darkness. On entering the cabinet, Miss Cook lies down upon the floor with her head on a pillow and is soon entranced.

"During the photographic séances, Katie muffled her medium's head up in a shawl to prevent the light falling upon her face. I frequently drew the curtain on one side when Katie was standing near, and it was a common thing for the seven or eight of us in the laboratory to see Miss Cook and Katie at the same time, under the full blaze of the electric light. We did not, on these occasions, actually see the face of the medium because of the shawl, but we saw her hands and feet; we saw her move uneasily under the influence of the intense light, and we heard her moan occasionally.

I have one photograph of the two together, but Katie is seated in front of Miss Cook's head. During the time I have taken an active part in these séances, Katie's confidence in me gradually grew, until she refused to take a séance unless I took charge of the arrangements. She said she always wanted me to keep close to her, and near the cabinet, and I found that after this confidence was established, and she was satisfied I would not break any promise I might make to her, the phenomena increased greatly in power, and tests were freely given that would have been unobtainable had I approached the subject in another manner. She often consulted me about persons present at the séance, and where they should be placed, for of late she had become very nervous, in consequence of certain ill-advised suggestions that force should be employed as an adjunct to more scientific modes of research."

This statement, by a scientist who in turn was President twice of the British Association and President of the Royal Society, might throw a little light into the minds of those who do not have his depth of understanding and his sympathetic nature for, after all, he was scientific in observing that honourable conduct produced conditions which led to outstanding results. In his photographic tests this was done: "One of the most interesting of the pictures is one in which I am standing by the side of Katie; she has her bare foot upon a particular part of the floor. Afterwards I dressed Miss Cook like Katie, placed her and myself in exactly the same position, and we were photographed by the same cameras placed exactly as in the other experiment, and illuminated by the same light. When these two pictures are placed over each other the two photographs of myself coincide exactly as regards stature, etc., but Katie is half a head taller than Miss Cook and looks a big woman in comparison with her. In the breadth of her face, in many of the pictures, she differs essentially in size from her medium, and the photographs show several other points of difference."

Then the great scientist who had begun so cautiously and had fared so well and had travelled so far, comes to this conclusion: "But photography is as inadequate to depict the perfect beauty of Katie's face, as words are powerless to describe her charm of manner. Photography may, indeed, give a map of her countenance; but how can it reproduce the brilliant purity of her complexion, or the ever-varying expression of her most noble features, now overshadowed with sadness, when relating some bitter experiences of her past life, now smiling with all the innocence of happy girlhood when she had collected my children around her, and was amusing them by recounting anecdotes of her adventures in India?"

At this point, Crookes, the master of science, breaks into poetry to express himself and goes on: "Having seen so much of Katie lately when she has been illuminated by the electric light, I am enabled to add to the points of difference between her and her medium. I have the most absolute certainty that Miss Cook and Katie are two separate individuals so far as their bodies are concerned. Several little marks on Miss Cook's face are absent on Katie's. Miss Cook's hair is so dark a brown as almost to appear black; a lock of Katie's which is now before me and which she allowed me to cut from her luxuriant tresses, having first traced it up to the scalp and satisfied myself that it actually grew there, is a rich golden auburn. One evening I timed Katie's pulse. It beat steadily at 75 whilst Miss Cook's pulse, a little time after, was going at its usual rate of 90. On applying my ear to Katie's chest I could hear a heart beating rhythmically inside, and pulsating even more steadily than did Miss Cook's heart when she allowed me to try a similar experiment after the séance. Tested in the same way, Katie's lungs were found to be sounder than her medium's, for at the time I tried my experiment, Miss Cook was under medical treatment for a severe cough.

"When the time came for Katie to take her farewell, I asked that she would let me see the last of her. Accordingly, when she had called each of the company up to her and had spoken to them a few words in private, she gave some general directions for the future guidance and protection of Miss Cook. From these, which were taken down in shorthand, I quote: 'Mr Crookes has done very well throughout, and I leave Florrie with the greatest confidence in his hands, feeling perfectly sure he will not abuse the trust I place in him. He can act in any emergency better than I can myself, for he has more strength.' Having concluded her directions, Katie invited me into the cabinet with her and allowed me to remain there to the end. After closing the curtain she conversed with me for some time, and then walked across the room to where Miss Cook was lying senseless upon the floor. Stooping over her, Katie touched her and said, 'Wake up, Florrie, wake up! I must leave you now.' Miss Cook then woke and tearfully entreated Katie to stay a little time longer. 'My dear, I can't. My work is done. God bless you,' Katie replied, and then continued speaking to Miss Cook. For several minutes the two were conversing with each other, till at last Miss Cook's tears prevented her speaking. Following Katie's instructions, I then came forward to support Miss Cook, who was falling on the floor, sobbing hysterically. I looked round, but the white-robed Katie had gone."

Crookes's comment on all this, after testifying to the conditions he was allowed to impose, is that Miss Cook was "open and straightforward in speech, and I have never seen anything approaching the slightest symptom of a wish to deceive. Indeed, I do not believe she could carry on a deception if she were to try. ... And to imagine that an innocent schoolgirl of 15 should be able to conceive and then successfully carry out for three years so gigantic an imposture, and in that time should submit to any test which might be imposed upon her, should bear the strictest scrutiny, should be willing to be searched at any time, either before or after a séance, and should meet with even better success in my own house than at that of her parents, knowing that she visited me with the express object of submitting to strict scientific tests—to imagine, I say, the Katie King of the last three years to be the result of imposture does more violence to one's reason and common sense than to believe her to be what she herself affirms."

And was Crookes a Spiritualist? Here is the evidence. After thanking Miss Cook's parents for their co-operation he says: "My thanks and those of all Spiritualists are also due to Mr Charles Blackburn for the generous manner in which he has made it possible for Miss Cook to devote her whole time to the development of these manifestations and latterly to their scientific examination."

I said I would list the honours which were conferred on Crookes in his scientific career. After he had sent to the Royal Society, in 1875, a paper on radiation, he was awarded a Royal Medal. In 1880 the French Academy of Science awarded him an extraordinary prize of 3,000 francs and a gold medal in recognition of his discoveries in molecular physics and radiant matter. For his researches on the behaviour of substances under the influence of electrical discharge in a high vacuum he was awarded the Davy Medal by the Royal Society in 1888. His official biographer, Sir William A. Tilden, F.R.S., says: "It would be almost impossible to enumerate all the various directions in which Sir William Crookes (he was knighted in 1897) occupied himself in connection with problems of public interest or as expert adviser to the government, but in passing may be mentioned his work on the disposal of town sewage, his reports on the composition and quality of daily samples of water supplied to London from 1880 to 1906, and his services as consulting expert on the Ordnance Board from 1907 onwards. Nor should it be forgotten that the officer or president of the Royal Society is, in many learned societies, no sinecure. In presiding over the Chemical Society, 1887-89, the Institution of Electrical Engineers, 1890-94, the British Association, 1898, the Society of Chemical Industry, 1913, and, finally, the Royal Society, 1913-15, Sir William paid close attention to all the multifarious details of the business of each society. He also served as honorary secretary to the Royal Institution from 1900 to 1913, and as foreign secretary of the Royal Society from 1908 to 1912. Every man of science among his contemporaries will be ready to affirm, therefore, that the numerous honours which were showered on

Crookes by the most distinguished academics and universities in the world were well-earned and very fittingly conferred. He received from the Royal Society the Royal, the Davy and the Copley medal, and from the Royal Society of Arts the Albert Medal, and finally, in 1910, the Order of Merit was conferred on him by the King."

He once showed, in South Africa, that the residue of cordite exploded in a closed sealed cylinder contained crystallised particles possessing the form of the diamond, and his views on the chemistry of wheat production are still such as to gain the respect of experts in that line. Tilden, who is not at all sympathetic to Spiritualism, says in conclusion: "And so the judgment of the contemporary generation of chemists must certainly place him in the front rank of scientific pioneers."

CHAPTER ELEVEN

EXPERIMENTS IN PSYCHIC STRUCTURES

WHILE Crookes in his researches with Florence Cook came to the conclusion that Katie King was a distinct entity separate from the medium and he had the courage, far ahead of his time, to say so and to defend his conclusions, he also paved the way for the investigations of a more detailed nature carried out by Dr. W. J. Crawford of Belfast, a mechanical engineer.

Crawford's three books, *Experiments in Psychical Science; The Reality of Psychic Phenomena*; and *Psychic Structures*; are in their way textbooks for scientific investigators. Yet Crawford says in *The Reality of Psychic Phenomena*: "I do not discuss in this book the question of the identity of the invisible operators. ... But in order that there may be no misapprehension, I wish to state explicitly that I am personally satisfied they are the spirits of human beings who have passed into the Beyond."

The mediumistic family with whom he sat were the Golighers, consisting of Kathleen, the principal medium, her three sisters, a young brother, father and brother-in-law. No researcher has excelled Crawford for thoroughness. He had the advantage, uncommon in this work, of a sympathetic nature. His passionate devotion to detail and ruthless analysis of results led him to the discovery that ectoplasm, that substance which is produced from the body of a physical medium when in a psychic state, is employed, so far as we know, in most instances where levitation, raps, knocks, the movement of objects at a distance from the medium, and other associated phenomena are produced.

This is what happened in a typical Goligher test sitting. The group met in a room almost devoid of furniture. When possible, photographs were taken, and after several years of co-operation between the scientist and all those concerned, a remarkable series of flashlight pictures resulted. In these, the whitish, billowing ectoplasm is seen mostly at the medium's feet, near the ankles and on the legs just below the knees. In others the ectoplasm is seen to have moved forward under the table, making the first attempts at what Crawford later discovered was a true cantilever action, which means that a straight rod protruding, say, from a wall, would extend for some distance, and be strong enough to support an object. This fascinated Crawford's engineering mind, and he proved his theory in a series of experiments in which so much force was applied to the table being held by the cantilever that the medium from whom it proceeded was moved. The structure could not be broken, or rather would not be broken, since Crawford was not the man to do anything violent, thereby destroying the aim he had in mind—to establish a basis for the mechanics of physical phenomena in the séance room.

After some years he came to the conclusion that the material of which he saw so much "closely resembles, if it is not identical with, the material used in all such materialisation phenomena. In fact, it is not too much to say that this whitish, translucent, nebulous matter is the basis of all psychical phenomena of the physical aura. Without it in some degree no physical phenomena are possible." In that he was scientifically affirming conclusions reached by Spiritualists in many parts of the world, though few of them had discovered the mode of operation laid bare by Crawford.

He also discovered in cases of levitation of objects where a great weight was to be moved that, instead of a cantilever, the psychic structure would pass from the medium along the floor and it has to be remembered that the cantilever does not at any point rest on the floor—turn at an angle, move up to the object to be lifted and then send a short supporting strut from near the point of turning to the floor. With this "edifice" erected, great lifting power could be passed to any object. Crawford did not in all his researches come any closer to the solution of the problem of how the energy is transmitted through the medium to the object. There were several other questions yet unanswered, but maybe another Crawford, Crookes or a Zöllner will arise who will carry his investigations a stage further. The problem is to discover how the ectoplasm is produced within the organism of the medium, how it is extruded, what is its nature at the moment of leaving the physical body, and how energy can be driven along its course so that raps, knocks and movements are produced at great speed.

Crawford explains that for the first few years of his investigations, great care had to be taken to see that photographs were taken while the psychic structures were not under any form of stress, for he found that, even with the spirit guides co-operating, when he took flashlight photographs, Kathleen Goligher's body would tremble violently and jerk spasmodically for ten minutes afterwards. This scientific fact should be an awful warning to those untrained investigators whose burning desire for what they call an "exposure" leads them to snatch at what they consider to be unsatisfactory materialisations.

The question is always asked why darkness is necessary. Crawford did not always find that so, but then he was unusual. He worked often in gaslight shaded by red glass, and he could see sufficiently when he required to see. He used enough light to be able to measure the increase or decrease in the weight of the medium to test whether the spirit guides could alter the weight of an object. Where light could not be employed he had other means of checking, such as electrical contacts through which a bell was rung immediately a test condition was broken. All this was done in the friendliest co-operation with the circle. It is an indispensable condition of psychic research at its best that there should be harmony in the circle. But to show the difference that darkness makes, he once sat with all light excluded and what followed he described as a "veritable earthquake." The room itself seemed to heave and jump and for the first time in all his hundreds of experiments he was glad when he could turn on the light. Those researchers who obtain the best results are those who treat the medium, not as an object, but as a human being who is naturally affected by the psychic conditions of the séances and who leave the results to be observed or recorded by instruments of the simplest nature. Crawford went over his experiments again and again and found as his reward, and at the end of years of work, he had the solid satisfaction of having made a most important contribution to a difficult and little understood branch of scientific investigation.

Non-Spiritualists have to realise that all this work is highly organised on the Other Side, and that those in charge of the Goligher circle were specially trained for the particular tasks they had to carry out, and that while they could answer most of the scientist's questions about the phenomena under observation, they could not go beyond that. I say this because it occurred to me that since he had so much success in one direction, his investigations were limited. Like everyone else in this world he, too, had his limitations. He intended to be unduly sceptical and critical of things he had not investigated and therefore did not understand. He had hoped, at one time, to obtain full materialisations in the Goligher circle, but these did not develop, the phenomena being confined almost solely to those which enabled objects to be lifted and, in general, to produce the results for which he was justly famed.

Among his discoveries were that the ectoplasmic rods used for producing raps could be rapidly varied in size, and that while the larger ones were soft to the touch the smaller could be almost instantly hardened until they felt like metal. Crawford was not of the opinion that he had seen everything connected with this type of phenomena and he thought that much that he was shown was for his instruction and that in other circumstances, and with other mediums, there were differences. He did not jump to the conclusion that because psychic structures began to form at Kate Goligher's feet, this would be true in all physical mediumship. For his instruction, the guides could make ectoplasm bounce like a rubber ball, make scraping and sawing noises, soft, hair-like touches and blows like those from a sledgehammer. He even devised a means of proving that his cantilever theory of levitation was true. At different times he had spring balances placed under the test table and while that was being raised, no change was recorded in the balance.

He found also in investigating the cantilever theory that when the medium was sitting on a weighing machine, while the table was levitated, its weight was added to that of the medium. To the mechanical engineer this was proof of the cantilever theory. This was further verified when the weight of the table was increased to such an extent that, instead of its being lifted by force issuing through the medium, she was raised or moved by the superior force exerted through the table. At other times, when the strut was employed, no amount of pressure exerted through the table caused any reaction to the medium.

He found that during the experiments to test the cantilever theory, the body of the medium was under stress, much as a piece of metal would be under stress in similar circumstances, though in her case the stress was observed in the iron-like stiffness of her muscles from wrist to shoulder. In case the ultra-sceptical are of opinion that the medium was, by tensing her muscles, raising the table, the answer is that she had no physical contact at all with the objects being lifted. The only time she was allowed to touch any object being moved was when Crawford wished to test what effect such a movement would have. And this was the result: the moment she touched an object being levitated or moved in any way, it either dropped to the floor or stopped its movement. Crawford also discovered that in his tests the psychic rod had a suction-like action at the point of contact with objects, for he and his collaborators often heard the scraping movement of the mushroom-like end feeling for a firm grip. The top part of the cantilever column would flatten out, something like a pancake. This was tested, not only with a table, but by Crawford asking the spirit operators to press against the sole of his raised foot so that he could feel the pressure being exerted. He said it felt thick, like a large pancake, and so much pressure was exerted that his foot and leg were pressed back, despite his resistance.

This discovery of the action of the cantilever and the other levers employed throws a new light on a most important subject. No one reading the conclusions of Crawford—and they should be studied by all who seek to investigate this subject—can fail to be impressed by his work. When you read his explanation, simple, clear and founded on well-known mechanical laws, you wonder why it was not all discovered before. But all truth moves in stages, and I think it would have been too much of a shock if, say, Professors Hare, Zöllner, and Crookes had not only made their own discoveries, but something akin to Crawford's as well, and published them in their own day. I do not think an evolving world can bear too much revolutionising truth at one time. The homeopathic dose is the best. Yet, it is a bitter reflection that in spite of all that these men of science have done, the illuminating facts of Spiritualism are still misrepresented by those who ought to know better, for they claim to be educated and often are in positions of public responsibility, as a result of which their pronouncements receive undue credence.

Crawford discovered that these psychic rods, though hard at the end where contact was made with physical objects, were softer elsewhere and that contraction and expansion was rapid, for he often felt it in process. The ends could be made flat or convex according to the will of the operators, could be made as rigid and hard as iron, or as soft as putty. What intrigued him to the very end was that while so much could be done to satisfy him, a physical experimenter, he never found what caused the psychic rod to cease to be material and then suddenly be invisible although pressure was still resisted, and force was still exerted. He says that these structures were not only visible but were often made so for his own purposes. He also found that these rods could vanish almost instantly.

With great patience he experimented while the psychic operators, through these rods, levitated the table and by degrees turned it completely over so that it was held upside down. The greatest difficulty was experienced when the table was at an angle of 45 degrees. That seemed to be the critical position, and there was a good deal of slipping and scraping by the ends of the psychic rods until it was passed. Sometimes in these experiments, while the sucker-like ends of the rods were slipping about seeking a new hold, the table would drop as much as six inches.

The spirit guides concerned explained that during this difficult feat they would make crossbars out of the psychic material to have a firmer grip, or if the table had a crossbar they would utilise that as well. This is what he says of these experiments: "I may also say that often ... I stood right over the table. The light permissible while this phenomenon was occurring was very often quite strong, and all the floor space and the medium were quite visible. The medium was sitting firmly on her chair with feet on the floor, while the table was tossing about in the air three feet or so in front of her."

Those who are wedded to the theory of fraud, conscious or unconscious, by physical mediums, would do well to consider what Crawford called the "clay test". He would place shallow pans filled with modeller's soft clay, and ask that the psychic structure should make marks in it. These marks he submitted to microscopic tests and found that, as the ectoplasm passed over the medium's stocking and was nearing its densest state, it took on the stocking marks and imprinted them on the soft clay. Sometimes the force was so great that strands of wool would be torn, and in other cases the mesh in one stocking pattern was permanently forced open showing that the passage of this now physical substance was marked by changes which the experienced expect but would cause the ignorant to suspect fraud. On its return journey the ectoplasm, still in a physical state, would carry with it particles of clay—or any other substance used for marking its path—and as it passed through lace-holes of shoes or boots and over the mesh of the stocking and became gradually less physical, the clay, or other marking material, naturally left traces behind.

Crawford also established that none of the marking material could possibly have been touched by the medium, for he applied the most stringent conditions, which included supplying stockings, painting the inside of shoes, seeing that the medium wore tightly-laced boots which fitted her feet as gloves to hands, and then encasing her feet in a box, the lid of which fitted closely round her legs. Yet, under these conditions outstanding phenomena resulted. Sometimes the modeller's clay would have a boot or a shoe mark showing that the ectoplasm carried with it the characteristic markings of the object over which it passed.

As another form of test Crawford carefully tied cord tightly round the medium's ankles, which he bound to the back bar of her chair, so that she could not get within 18 inches of the clay. The strings and knots were always found intact at the end of the séances. Her chair remained stationary the whole time. As an extra precaution he tied the legs of all the sitters to their chairs and linked a binding material from one to the other so that one movement would be felt by all. He discovered later that there was no need for this elaborate precaution since all the phenomena of that kind came from the medium.

In no instance in the Goligher circle was there ever the slightest suggestion that any result was due to fraud. All kinds of marks were made but none of them could have come, or did come, from the medium's shoes because, as has been stated, the clay was either too far away for her to reach it, or her feet were controlled by being locked in a box or in some other fashion. Nearly all these marks, which varied from the size of one that could be made by a finger to one of four or five square inches, were covered with the imprint of stocking fabric. But when he requested it, Crawford obtained markings without the stocking fabric. He found that there was always a stocking marking on the clay at nearly all séances where the medium wore stockings. He discovered by microscopic examination that the psychic imprints made on the clay were altogether sharper than those which could be made normally by stockinged feet. He tested this, and he went into great detail to show how the psychic matter in a fluid state was put through a complicated process to make an impression on the clay.

During rapping, he put his hands in front of the medium's feet and ankles and distinctly felt the cold breeze of which other scientists have spoken. He describes it as a "kind of breeze which appeared to be caused by material particles of a cold, disagreeable, spore-like matter. There was no solid body whatever beyond her ankle where I intercepted the flow of these particles, but nevertheless they were an integral part of the rapping rod, for immediately I intercepted them the rapping ceased and could not be resumed for quite a long period of time." He even heard peculiar noises round the medium's feet and ankles before phenomena occurred, and his opinion is that the spasms in which they occurred were caused by the ectoplasm being sent in surges over the material of the stockings. He suggests that some flapping noises he heard on the floor were caused by the ectoplasm being removed from the medium's body.

He carried out many tests to show that none of the marks could have been made by the medium's feet, apart altogether from the fact that they were locked in a box. He even tried a test apparatus which the medium had constantly to press with her feet to prevent an alarm bell ringing. Even a small spasmodic movement of the feet would have rung the bell. Under this precaution a letter balance was moved up and down when it was so far away from the medium that she could not possibly have touched it. Crawford says that in some of these experiments the operators had difficulty in overcoming the test conditions, and that often while they were trying to satisfy him the test bells would ring. Yet, nearly always, they were successful in the end. Not only was the medium affected, as he found, by flashlight photographs, but the psychic structures themselves were acutely sensitive to light, and he comments that this conclusion was also reached in thousands of circles held by mediums throughout the world.

It was not until nearly the end of his experiments that he was able to examine the psychic structures in the Goligher circle. The apparatus was simple. He painted a sheet of cardboard with luminous paint and exposed it to the sunlight for some time. This cardboard was placed on the floor of the séance room and it glowed phosphorescently while he carried out his observations. It is significant that this occurred towards the end of his researches when the phenomena would be strong, the conditions stabilised, and the operators and the circle wholly confident of the scientist. The next stage was to lock the medium's feet in a box and to ask the operators to try and bring out a psychic structure. Soon a curved body, something like the toe of a boot, moved several times over the glowing cardboard as though testing the effect of light, and then moved freely about. This psychic structure, he found, resembled the front part of the human foot, but without the heel, was capable of amazingly rapid changes of form, and he watched different shapes being made—from a fine point to a hook-like end which could twist round objects such as a table leg. One end could be broadened out with an irregular edge like a cabbage leaf, while the other side would bulge. The flexibility of this structure he describes as "marvellous."

He also discovered that the more phosphorescent light he introduced, the more solid the structures had to become before he could examine them. During the photographic experiments Crawford's scientific colleagues remarked that it was striking how the psychic structure, without anybody asking, was placed directly in his line of sight. As this structure returned to the medium's body, Crawford could feel her shuddering. When a second photograph was taken the photographer requested mentally that the structure should remain in position for a minute and he counted the seconds mentally. He says that exactly at the 60th second the structure disappeared, and when it returned to the medium, she shivered most violently. Crawford put this down to the fact that the light affected the substance.

In other tests, carmine powder was carefully spread on garments worn by the medium to mark the journey of the ectoplasm from her body and back again. This was done many times, showed that the substance came from the trunk or body, moved down the stockings, scraping along them, entered the shoe, passed round the foot of the medium, and exhibited a strong, tearing action. Similar tests were carried out with a strong solution of methylene blue being rubbed on the inside of underwear, while damp carmine was rubbed on the stockings six inches above the shoe.

"When the séance was over," writes Crawford, "it was found that the methylene blue had been drawn downwards and upwards to the junction of the legs with the trunk. The carmine was traced down to the toes of both stockings. Test after test was made to show the line taken by the ectoplasm and the route of its return to the medium's body. Then a medical test was carried out by a doctor in which, while a wooden frame was placed round the medium's legs to prevent any movement in the direction of the table, her pulse was taken just before the phenomena started. It was 72, temperature 98.0, and respiration normal. Levitation went on while the doctor took the medium's pulse, sometimes from the wrist, sometimes from the neck. It was found that during levitation her pulse went up to 90 and once to 110, and that after the levitation, it fell slowly. Respiration was always normal, and the temperature rose to 98.4. The pulses of all the other sitters were found to be normal."

Other observations resulted in the discovery that during the extrusion of ectoplasm the medium's body underwent strong muscular movements and that "there was evidence that the fleshy part of the body from the waist downward decreased in size." He found that the "plasma", as he calls it, was not always white; sometimes it was dark and even black, but occasionally it would issue from the medium's chest, and that it could be made to do almost everything to prove the reality of the existence of psychic structures.

CHAPTER TWELVE

INSTRUCTION FROM BEYOND

PSYCHIC raps have been heard hundreds of thousands of times in this world, yet no one has investigated the method of their production with the thoroughness of Crawford. First, he discovered that the medium decreased in weight by eight pounds during experiments in making raps. As they increased in loudness so did the medium's weight decrease until, when blows of sledgehammer force were being delivered, the weight became stationary and remained steady to the end. He concluded that the intensity of the raps followed a proportional decrease in the weight of the medium and that no raps were produced without a loss of weight.

He found that all phenomena required a degree of preparation, that as soon as some weight was drawn from the medium it was easier to begin, and that when a specially loud blow was delivered on the floor the weighing machine would register a drop in weight of 20 lbs or more, and that immediately afterwards a slow return of the weight began, requiring six or seven seconds to complete the process. This indicated the ignorant nature of those sudden seizures of psychic structures by "researchers" at physical séances, these violent actions causing the ectoplasm to rush back into the medium's body with a force that produces sometimes even the marks of burning.

Crawford found that the spirit operators were as keen as he was on accurate results and did all they could to provide conditions in which observation would be reliable. There were no "tricks", such as manipulating the weighing machine to produce the idea of a loss in weight when all that might have happened was pressure on a balance. He also discovered that it took time to change from one kind of phenomenon to another, and that when heavy blows were being delivered the medium would rock backwards as though being struck by an object moving at considerable speed. He even saw the medium rocking backwards and forwards as though she were being struck like a punch-ball, and it appeared that the reaction was recoiling on her. His theory was that raps were produced by psychic, semiflexible rods projected from the body of the medium, each one becoming rigid near its extremity. His view was that this rigidity was brought about by a molecular action, that is to say, a stream of electrons passed along the rod at the will of the spirit operator, causing it to move and produce the desired sound.

He was convinced that the psychic touches felt at séances were done by means of these rods and that where softer noises are produced these were caused by rods passing over objects with rigid surfaces. In the case of the imitation of the sound of sandpaper being rubbed on the floor, he thought this was done by rubbing a soft part of the rod on a floorboard. The sound of a bouncing ball was easily imitated, but he admitted that the imitation of sawing a piece of wood was difficult to explain unless a psychic rod was moved across a piece of wood. The movement of small objects without physical contact he considered was due to these small psychic rods holding them, probably by adhesion.

It was noticed, he remarks, that when a small bell was lifted by this means the sound was dulled as though it were being held. He even went to the length of placing a typewriter in a circle and asking the operators to tap the keys. After some jamming on an old type of machine, they succeeded. For his benefit, fingerprints, enlarged to three times the normal size, were made on putty, and when he questioned the psychic operators on how it was done, they said that usually in rapping fingerprints were not used, and that a simple projection was employed. He experimented to test the delicacy of touch through these psychic rods and found they could cause an electroscope to discharge its quota of power, and that fluorescence could be dispelled from an X-ray screen.

Psychic photographs at one remarkable séance showed that from each of the sitters there came a stream of psychic stuff which joined into a column rising vertically into the air for about a height of five feet from the floor. Projecting from the medium was another bar of this material which met the psychic energy as it returned from the top of the column. This photograph, according to Crawford, showed much of the mechanism of levitation. He described the structure as a kind of psychic pump along which the energy flowed. The psychic operator said in reply to his questions that they had caused the picture of the structure to appear on the plate because they wished to show him how the psychic fluid circulated while physical phenomena were being produced. They said that an arch came from each sitter, but that the strongest one emerged from the medium, and that all the time the energy was circulating. They also said that during levitation this pump was one of the means whereby objects were raised, while the other methods of the cantilever and the rod were still in operation.

Crawford found, too, that the net loss of weight from the medium at a sitting would be no more than two ounces. He did not, at any time, discover the nature of the force which, he said, appeared to operate with a molecular action, although he had clairvoyants at séances to see what information could be gathered. All they did was to confirm his views of the structure required to raise an object. To probe this matter as far as he could, Miss Goligher went into trance and one of her guides, who said he had been a doctor on earth, answered Crawford's questions as well as he could. He said that two kinds of substance were used for the experiments, one being taken in comparatively large quantities from the medium and sitters. Nearly all of this was returned at the close of a séance. The other substance was taken in very small quantities only from the medium. This could not be returned since it consisted of a substance extracted from the interior of the medium's nerve cells. Once used for the purposes of phenomena it could not be returned, said the doctor, as its structure was broken up. Crawford neither confirmed nor denied this statement, but he gave it as a matter of interest.

Of the operators themselves he said that all their answers were given firmly, whether they were in agreement or disagreement with him. Not once did he find that they said they could do something and failed to do it. His experiments showed that things were as they said they would be. The only one to give him any information without it being sought was in the case of the doctor just quoted. This entity gave instructions for conducting physical séances and explained why hands should be held, for it shortened the period of preparation and paved the way for the phenomena in the second half of a sitting. Crawford found that holding hands and sitting in a circle was equivalent to charging a tank with liquid so that a pump could work well. In the case of the Golighers the visible effect of the perfect working of this "pump" was the spasmodic jerkings of the sitters' bodies.

Having gone so far, Crawford speculated on the kind of energy behind all the phenomena. He did not know, but from observation his theory was that it was a form of chemical energy associated with the human nervous system. He found that the cold wind at the beginning of the séance was due to material being evaporated from the bodies of the sitters and that particles of matter were being extruded at the same time. He thought that the operators on the Other Side drew off molecules from the nervous system, from the wrists, the hands, fingers or other parts of the body and that these particles, having a considerable amount of latent energy, could act on anything they contacted. He theorised that as this energy passed round the circle, it received an increase or additional impulse of energy from the medium and collected power until that point was reached when the guides were ready to begin their work.

Having exacted from the medium the small quantity of nervous substance necessary to complete the reservoir of power, the séance began properly, and the task commenced of drawing semi-physical ectoplasm from the medium to produce all the wonderful phenomena of the séance room.

CHAPTER THIRTEEN

LODGE'S GREAT CONTRIBUTION

SIR OLIVER LODGE was, to the ordinary man, perhaps the ideal scientist. He did great things and was simple. He was celebrated all over the world, yet he was a family man. He was equally at home in the laboratory, in discussing the problems of investigating the atom, and in giving kindly, warm, fatherly advice based on his Spiritualist experiences to those who were depressed and burdened by the world. In 1914, in his presidential address to the British Association, he summed up his views by saying that psychic investigation had convinced him that "memory and affection are not limited to that association with matter by which alone they can manifest themselves here and now, and that personality persists beyond bodily death."

It can no longer be doubted, even by the most wilful sceptic, that sufficient men of standing in physical science have investigated to the best of their ability and present-day knowledge, and have been convinced that the fundamental claim of Spiritualism is true—that human personality survives bodily death, that consciousness far transcends our earthly expression of it, that memory, likes, idiosyncrasies, dislikes, affection and love are carried with us into the spirit world, the existence of which is now as rationally proved as is Newton's law of gravity.

It was alleged in his lifetime, by those who sought to throw any discredit upon Lodge, that he came to investigate Spiritualism in his very old age when, it was assumed, his powers were failing. It was also said that mourning for his son Raymond, who was killed in the last war, set him off on the quest of consolation. That was not so. He began his psychic investigations in 1883 and wrote an account of his experiences in 1908.

He wrote several books on psychic subjects, but the best known was *Raymond*, the account of his son's proof of his own survival. The medium through whom this was proved was Mrs Leonore Piper, an American. To understand the kind of instrument Lodge employed in this phase of his investigation I give this summary of Mrs Piper's powers. She was tested by Professor Hyslop, who had the Chair of Logic and Ethics at Columbia University, New York, where he was later Principal. Mrs Piper had been discovered by Professor William James of Harvard, the brother of Henry James, the litterateur. William James found that Mrs Piper suffered from lapses from the normal, and during certain states of consciousness her family accidentally discovered that she could reveal things which could not have come from any living person. James communicated with Dr Richard Hodgson, an English psychologist then living in Boston, and the test they devised sounds comical at this date.

Professor Hyslop wore a mask which covered him from forehead to below his beard. He disguised his voice, did not give his name, and entered Mrs Piper's home unannounced, going into her presence only when she was entranced. Mrs Piper did not at any time see his features, hear his voice, or even glimpse his beard. During these tests Hyslop said that she wrote a secret password from his dead father, a word which was unknown to anyone else in the world. When she was entranced her head rested on pillows on a stand in front of her, and her head was turned aside so that she could not see the writing that was being done through her right hand. Mrs Piper would talk normally until she fell forward on the pillows and her trance state began. Professor Hyslop began by being sceptical, but he had scores of messages through this medium who submitted to medical tests during her séances and, in the end, convinced him.

Afterwards she was invited to go to London to be tested by researchers, stopping at Liverpool on the way to give sittings to Lodge. But before this, Lodge said he had received a message from F. W. H. Myers, the famous scholar, through Mrs Piper, who was at that time in America. The message was transmitted to the medium by Hodgson, who had then passed on. The message from Myers had a classical allusion which Lodge had verified and amplified. It came from one of the odes of Horace, and it was a warning of some blow to come. Myers hinted in the message, through the classical allusion, that he would try to protect Lodge, probably from over-grieving at the death of his son.

The message was received on September 6, 1915, while Lodge was in Scotland. His son, Raymond, was killed near Ypres on September 14 and the father was officially informed the next day. To test further the classical reference in the Myers message, Lodge asked other scholars and they all referred him to the ode in Horace from which his first authority had quoted. To show that Lodge appreciated the difficulties of ordinary people in seeking evidence of Survival, he says that good mediums resent the slightest clue being given at séances, and adds: "It is practically impossible for mediums to hunt up and become normally acquainted with the family history of their numerous sitters, and those who know them are well aware that they do nothing of the sort; but in making arrangements for a sitting, it is not easy unless special precautions are taken to avoid giving a name and address, and thereby appearing to give facilities for fraud. In our case, and in that of our immediate friends, precautions to secure complete anonymity were taken—sometimes in a rather elaborate manner."

Bearing that in mind, consider what happened. Eight days after official receipt of news of the passing of Raymond, Lady Lodge had an anonymous sitting with the well-known medium, Mrs Osborne Leonard, who was a stranger to her. A friend had booked the sitting. A message was spelt out by tilts of the table: "Tell father I have met some friends of his." When asked if names could be given, the reply was, "Yes, Myers." Two days later, Lodge had his first sitting with Mrs Leonard, who had not seen him before. This séance was also arranged anonymously. Mrs Osborne Leonard explained that her spirit control was a young girl named Feda, who brought messages. The medium was entranced and Feda gave a detailed description of a young man. Raymond's work was described as that of helping other young men who had passed over in battle but were not aware of it, and then he gave a phrase which reminded Lodge of something his son had written in a letter from the front.

That same afternoon Lady Lodge had her first sitting with the medium Vout Peters, to whom she was a stranger. The scientist gives a detailed account of this sitting which contained evidence about Myers and his son, and ended dramatically with the medium jumping up in his chair, snapping his fingers excitedly and speaking out loudly: "Good God! How father will be able to speak out! Much firmer than he has ever done, because it will touch our hearts." Earlier in the sitting, there was a statement: "Hitherto it has been a thing of the head, now I am come over it is a thing of the heart."

The Lodges sat often with mediums thereafter, and at one séance with Vout Peters, his first with that medium, Raymond in urging his father to proclaim his proof of Survival said: "For God's sake, father, do it. Because if you only knew and could only see what I see; hundreds of men and women heartbroken, and if you could only see the boys on our side shut out, you would throw the whole strength of yourself into this work, but you can do it."

The guide said that Raymond was so emotional and filled with the desire to speak with his father that he wanted to control the medium, but that could not be allowed because he was not then trained to do it. After some difficulty the guide gave a further message from Raymond, who said that by his passing away many hundreds would benefit. Now that was fulfilled, because *Raymond* was, in its day of popularity, one of the most widely discussed Spiritualist books, and all because of one statement, that in the spirit world some people could have cigars and whisky, if they so desired. That upset all those brought up in the conventional idea that when you die you pass into a heaven of harps and angels or into a hell of fires and devils. The statement occurred after Raymond had become skilled in communication.

Lodge was sitting with Mrs Osborne Leonard whose control, Feda, was reporting what the young man said. Raymond was trying to give his father a picture of that part of the spirit world inhabited by men and women who had just passed over. "People here," said Feda, relaying Raymond's statements, "try to provide everything that is wanted. A chap came over the other day who would have a cigar. 'That's finished them,' he thought. He means he thought they would never be able to provide that. But there are laboratories over here, and they manufacture all sorts of things in them. Not like you do out of solid matter, but out of essences, and ethers, and gases. It's not the same as on the earth plane, but they were able to manufacture what looked like a cigar. He didn't try one himself, because he didn't care to; you know he wouldn't want to"—that is, Raymond would not want to, for Feda is still reporting his statement.

"But the other chap jumped at it. But when he began to smoke it, he didn't think so much of it; he had four altogether, and now he doesn't look at one. They don't seem to get the same satisfaction out of it, so gradually it seems to drop from them. But when they first come, they do want things. Some want meat, and some strong drink; they call for whisky sodas. Don't think I am stretching it, when I tell you that they can manufacture even that. But when they have had one or two, they don't seem to want it so much-not those that are near here. He has heard of drunkards who want it for months and years over here, but he hasn't seen any. Those I have seen, he says, don't want it any more—like himself with his suit, he could dispense with it under the new conditions. He wants people to realise that it is just as natural as on the earth plane."

Father and son discussed the best kind of proof of Survival. The young man was in the difficulty of all communicators, saying that he was divided between the desire to give objective proof of materialisation and direct voice. He also detailed information about his life in the spirit world. The scientist, in a summary of some of these séances, admits that even a detailed account is a poor substitute for the actual experience. When Lodge received the printer's proofs of *Raymond*, it was pointed out to him that the statements about cigars and whisky would start controversy and he was advised to strike them out. But he refused, saying: "It's true." His mind was as simple as that. His view was that even indiscretions should be published because they indicated the kind of personality who was communicating.

Then Lodge had his own home circle, and he says of the séances: "After a time some messages were received, and family communications without any outside medium have gradually become easy." Some of the things that happened at these family séances were confirmed and commented upon by Raymond when his father sat with other mediums. In all, when you read carefully through this book *Raymond* and note the hundreds of evidential facts given by a devoted son to a loving father, you realise more and more that, for all Lodge's scientific discoveries, possibly the greatest he made was that communication between the living and the dead is simple and natural. This great man, whose towering intellect could range from the problems of atomic physics to speculations about the nature of that mysterious ether which he claimed accounts for much that happens in the universe, shows his almost schoolboyish excitement in *Raymond* when he describes a test which he calls the Honolulu incident.

His son Alec was in Birmingham and took some of his sitters home to the Lodge dwelling for a family sitting which lasted about ten minutes. The young people decided to ask Raymond to get Feda to say the word "Honolulu" to two other members of the family, Lionel and Norah, who that day were having a séance with Mrs Osborne Leonard. The three Lodge children, after their table sitting at home, wrote out a statement that they had decided on the Honolulu test phrase after 12 o'clock midday. A note was written on the back that the letter was posted at Birmingham Post Office at 12.43, and Sir Oliver noted that he received it at 7 p.m. The sitters in London knew nothing of the test and did not see anything unusual at the séance, because they did not think it was a good one. Because of that they made no report to the family until they returned from a holiday at Eastbourne a week later.

At the London sitting, Feda was giving evidence about some spirit people when she broke in to relay a message from Raymond who wanted her to ask them whether they could play "Honolulu." The control said that Raymond was roaring with laughter to show he was pleased about something. Sir Oliver says the three points in the Honolulu episode are: "Because it establishes a reality about the home sittings, because it so entirely eliminates anything of the nature of collusion, conscious or unconscious, because the whole circumstances of the test make it an exceedingly good one." He suggests that it was a case of telepathy carried out by a spirit messenger.

Mrs Osborne Leonard visited the Lodge home near Birmingham where Sir Oliver was Principal of the university, and Raymond repeated, at a sitting for his family, some of his imitations of Sir Herbert Tree, the famous actor, who was a frequent visitor at the Lodge home. Lady Lodge said that her son's humorous imitation conveyed through the medium intensely brought Raymond to her. These sittings with the medium in his own home convinced the scientist of the fact that people who have passed over remain themselves and retain their memories in spite of having left their bodies. This was borne in on him by a large number of little things which sceptics call trivial but when added up in their total amount to conclusive evidence.

Lady Lodge and one of her daughters, who appeared to be psychic, heard Raymond's voice at a sitting in a doctor's home near Birmingham, and there was a reference to it by the young man when he spoke through Feda to Sir Oliver and his wife three weeks later. Lady Lodge had a striking experience in America when she met a famous but unnamed author who said that a psychic happening changed his life "much as the vision on the road to Damascus changed the life of Paul." This experience left the author with psychic power and with a faculty, of which I have not heard before, called "auto-speech." Lady Lodge describes it: "I asked him to give me an example of this if he could. We were sitting a little apart from the three other people present, though within their hearing, and he very kindly let himself go. He just let his mouth stay open, and, without using lips or tongue, a voice came through him, and I felt certain Raymond spoke. I did not take it down, and it was nothing clearly evidential, but it was just the kind of thing Raymond is accustomed to say to me and was said in the way he says it."

When the Lodges returned to London, there was a sitting with Mrs Osborne Leonard at which Feda relayed Raymond's message: "Now to go back to the man who opened his mouth. It was very much the same kind of thing as trumpet mediumship. Both have the same source. In trumpet mediumship the voice, though seemingly independent of the medium, is connected in some way with the throat and larynx of the medium, and that is why tones of the medium's voice come in, and why it is so often coloured by the medium. It's not really independent. I've got tired of it lately."

Lodge was concerned, in discussions with Myers, to know whether some scientific facts could not be given through mediums. The famous scholar replied that it was much easier to present ideas, classical allusions and poetry than to put over statements of fact, except where there was a highly trained medium. But, of course, the aim of those on the Other Side who have charge of that organisation, which presents evidence at séances of all kinds, is not to tell scientists of facts which they will come to learn for themselves by their own investigations, but rather to present to individuals who mourn or who are in distress a body of ideas which will help them to remake their lives on the basis of spirit teaching.

I found little record of Lodge's sittings with physical mediums, but he has publicly stated: "I have seen a medium exert herself, and each time a thing at a distance was moved as if a rod had been pushed. But no rod was visible. The link was not made of ordinary matter. The physiologists are beginning to think that that they find the link in ectoplasm, and certainly some of these things are done by a material emanation from the medium, controlled in some way we do not understand, controlled intelligently to be able to transmit force—at least to be able to do many things, to mould itself into various shapes, and, I believe, to transmit force." He said this in exposition of the theory of the ether of space, of which he was a tireless teacher. This theory has been discussed throughout the ages and many outstanding philosophers and scientists have accepted it as a working hypothesis to explain the phenomena of heat and light.

Lodge's view of ether is worth noting because he gives some of its properties-that it fills all space in the most thorough manner, is absolutely cold and transparent, cannot be dispersed, is not viscous, is the sole vehicle of radiation, light, X-rays, wireless waves, and that electric and magnetic fields are forms of energy existing in it. He asserts: "The ether is indirectly responsible for all physical and chemical activity. What other function this universal medium may be found to possess, and whether light and mind can be in any way associated with those functions, it must be left to posterity to find out."

This scientist, who did as much as any man to perfect the basic discoveries on which modern wireless, television and radiolocation depend, was more interested in his theory of ether than in his discoveries in radio. He was often challenged about the spirit opinion of his scientific theories and he said that those whom he had contacted on the Other Side encouraged him in the view he took of ether. He has stated—and I quote this as evidence of the intellect of one more scientist, justly world famous, who proved Spiritualism to be true: "I would define matter as that which is capable of locomotion. The notion of rest is an illusion. No piece of matter is at rest. All matter is moving. The ether is the link between mind and matter. There is a body of matter and a body of ether. The two are inseparable. When I use this term 'ether,' I am speaking of that which has been my life study. All the properties we have discovered with regard to the ether show it to be perfect, that is why it is so difficult to experiment upon it."

This man, who towered above most of his scientific contemporaries in his perception of fundamentals, and excelled all of them with his gift of popular exposition, said also—and again I am quoting for the benefit of inquirers and sceptics to show the kind of intellect he possessed: "It (ether) is elusive. You cannot get at it. So much so that there are some who have tried to believe that it does not exist; by which they only mean that it eludes all their senses, and they do not mean to attend to anything except that which they can see by their senses. They say they will not mention the ether until they can be given it to handle, and they cannot touch it. But we know it is responsible for electricity, for magnetism, and for light; for gravitation also, through the work of Einstein. It is also responsible for cohesion. I have to explain why those particles hold together. My eldest son, when he was a small urchin, said to me: 'Father, when you pick up one end of a stick, why does the rest of the stick come up, too?'

"I was quite pleased with that question, for I could not answer it at that time. There are a lot of ordinary things you cannot answer. We do not know why a thing drops, and it may be sufficient as a popular statement that the ether presses it down. Newton knew that he had not worked it out. A little while ago we had not worked out cohesion"—and Lodge was the coinventor of the coherer, one of the principal devices in the development of radio and other electrical appliances. "Now we know it to be magnetic, electric. These things hang together by the electrical forces which connect them entirely in the ether. The ether does a lot more than people know. And we have got to think about it if we are to complete a philosophy."

Nearly everything that Lodge said in defence of his theory of ether could be quoted in support of the statements about the existence of spirit people and a spirit world, but of them we have more tangible evidence than we have of the ether of space. What Lodge declared without qualification on ether, he also said without restraint about spirit existence and the fact of communication between this world and the next. Matter to him was only a slight modification of ether, so slight in fact that to a being in the other world it might also seem to be beneath his attention. Yet to us, unless we have a spirit view of life, it is predominant.

In his book *My Philosophy*, in the section devoted to "The Evidence for Survival and its Mechanism" he writes: "It is really my pronouncement, probably my final pronouncement to the world, as to what I think of things in general. Basing my conclusions on experience, I am absolutely convinced, not only of Survival, but of demonstrated Survival." And in 1934, the man who had helped to bring about radio, broadcast to the world how he received communications from dead members of his own family in 1889, and how later, in 1901, he received from F. W. H. Myers a series of messages and cross-correspondences interwoven with scholarship and classical learning, a knowledge far beyond the education of the medium. He was, when he broadcast, 82 years old, and did not hesitate to criticise official science for its unscientific attitude towards psychic facts.

He was merely repeating what has been stated by every scientist with whom this book deals, for they were men ahead, far ahead, of the scientific orthodoxies of their time. Lodge thought it was his last talk. It was indeed his last wireless talk. This man, patiently waiting to pass over to the Other Side after a long and noble life   in the service of humanity, said this of his belief that love bridges the chasm between this world and the next:

"I did not arrive at this belief by a religious channel. My own belief was based on the facts and experiences studied in the large and comprehensive science which, in my view, should take into account the whole of the phenomena and not limit itself to material phenomena, as urged by leaders of the 19th century and fashionable among most scientific men since Sir Isaac Newton."

At the end of his broadcast he gave this message of comfort to many millions who were rightly looking to this elder of the human race for something on which they could rely: "Let me take advantage of this unique opportunity. Let me speak to those who find life hard, who get depressed sometimes and wonder whether all the struggle and effort are worthwhile. Let me convey to them some assurance and state the certainty which has gradually grown up in my mind as the result of all the evidence obtained over a period of nearly fifty years. All this evidence, so full and unmistakable, has brought me to the perception that the spiritual world is a great reality, and has led me back to a realisation of the truth of the utterances attributed to the founder of Christianity, 'In my Father's house are many mansions. If it were not so, I would have told you. I go to prepare a place for you.'

"We are no different, the moment we pass over. Our friends come to welcome us when we cross the barrier. I constantly receive letters from bereaved people who are in deep distress at the loss of a child or a young person. I can only pass on the information that has been vouchsafed to me and assure them that all is well with their loved ones. The children are taken care of by good people. The veil between the two worlds is wearing thin. It is possible, given the right conditions, to communicate with those we call the dead. They are still mindful of our love for them and they reciprocate it fully. They are hurt by our excessive grief. They do not think of themselves as dead, but as fully alive, free of the clogging body, and able to move freely in their new state, using the etheric body which they possessed all the time."

Lodge never tired of explaining to people who wrote to him asking, not for his views on the ether of space, but on the means whereby they could reach their loved ones, that the apparently trivial messages were the important ones. He told, again and again, how in his own home circle, little things that were known to the family would be used by Raymond to put over points of evidence which in the total were impressive. "I know," he once wrote, "that I am helped continually by those on the Other Side. I am grateful to those higher powers who have led me thus to become convinced of the reality of the spiritual world."

Lodge's life was not always lived on the Olympian heights where scientific opinions and philosophic detachment are the sole means of expression. He took his B.Sc. degree as the result of studies at night classes, and he gained honours in physics. Then he took his D.Sc. and became Professor of Physics, University College, Liverpool, where he stayed for nine years. He was awarded, in 1898, the Rumford Medal by the Royal Society. He was Principal of Birmingham University from its establishment in 1900 to 1919. He was knighted in 1902 and in the next year became Romanes Lecturer at Oxford, and was for two years President of the British Association.

Quotations from Lodge's views on Spiritualism would occupy a whole book, but whenever he went to a developed medium his son Raymond was there with some fresh evidence, and if, at times, the power was weak he would refer to it in the home circle, or through another medium, to explain why results were inadequate. Lodge summed it all up in this way: "The things to be investigated are either true or false. If false, pertinacious inquiry will reveal their falsity. If true, they are profoundly important, for there are no half-truths in nature; every smallest new departure has portentous consequences; our eyes must open slowly, or we should be overwhelmed." And he helped to open the eyes of the world a little more.

Lodge's Spiritualist friend, J. Arthur Hill, who made a selection of the letters which they exchanged over twenty years on psychic and other matters, shows in his book that Lodge had a deeper understanding even of the psychological aspects of mediumship than many psychologists regarded as being leading psychic researchers. He had even stumbled upon the clue that guides do make use of the subconscious minds of mediums for certain work, although he did not elaborate that since he did not have a great deal of experience of the phenomena of trance. Lodge disclaimed extensive possession of the faculty of intuition, but for me, at least, he indicates that when it did operate this prompting of the spirit led him to valuable research, not all of which was appreciated in his time. Personal letters are more revealing than a formal autobiography, since they reflect the changing moods and ideas of the writer. In his letters, Lodge unconsciously exposes the limitations of scientists, especially in his own day. The letters also reveal his own gradual emergence from the standpoint of a cold-blooded investigator to that of a leading exponent of the truth of Survival.

He describes a council meeting of the British Association in London, and tells how, when they were discussing the choice of a President, someone brought up the question of the sub-section on psychology which had branched off from the section on physiology. Professor Vernon Harcourt, F.R.S., a chemist, asked how psychology came to be associated with physiology and how it got into the programme of the British Association. Lodge was carrying on a whispered conversation with Crookes at the time and did not catch the exact words. But the drift of the discussion became clear when the Vice-Chancellor of Manchester University, who was a botanist, said that in Manchester they had a lecturer in experimental psychology who used a laboratory, and that it was quite an orthodox subject. Then a physiologist explained that the psychology dealt with in their sub-section had nothing to do with psychical research. An official of the Association chimed in: "Oh, it has nothing to do with psychical research or ghosts. Psychical research is a misnomer, because there is no research in it." From that, Lodge said it was clear that anything to do with psychical research was forbidden. This discussion impressed him; that is why he noted it as being typical of the attitude of scientific men of his day, and he might have added, of any other day.

His comment is: "The general ignorance of some scientific men certainly does amaze me; but to taboo psychology because of our recent unorthodox investigations goes beyond what I should have anticipated. And even the botanist of Manchester, to whom I afterwards spoke, seemed to associate the term psychology with the experimental branch of that subject, though he also remembered that it was included in the professorial chair of philosophy. I fully expect that attempts will be made from time to time to terminate the existence of the young subsection, for fear it should blossom into a section full-blown, as physiology itself did about ten years ago. I cannot say that I am proud of the average scientific man at the present time; fortunately there are some exceptions."

Nothing indicates Lodge's nobility of nature more markedly than the detachment with which he received criticism and handled his detractors. In another letter to Hill he says: "That my occasional psychic utterances do harm to my scientific reputation—even so far as causing some of them to think me more or less cracked—is manifest, for I have many signs of that."

He who saw so clearly in the scientific fields in which he was eminent saw equally clearly in Spiritualism. For although he did not wholly subscribe to its religious implications, he had grasped sufficient of the fundamentals to detect the flaws in every alternative hypothesis presented to him. He said that this was true of Maeterlinck's theories, and he had progressed so far as to realise the importance of the truth that there are many cases of phenomena which could be explained by the fact of spirit possession, even for a short time. It is the mark and sign of outstanding men and women that they either overestimate, as they must do, their own achievements or they go to the other extreme of self-detraction. Nowhere is the former case clearer than when Lodge is discussing his own work in science, and when he states, without prompting or any observable reason, that the young men who were then rising had far outdistanced him and his contemporaries in physics. He reports this with a selflessness so unusual in this world that I am compelled to remark on it.

And in the same almost spiritual detachment, he dealt with psychic questions put to him. He discussed with Hill the problem of preparing test questions to leave behind when he died so that he could, by giving the answers to them through a strange medium, prove his survival even to psychic researchers. He had thought about many phases of mediumship apart from the physical, in which he had experiences with Margery Crandon, the Boston medium who, with her husband, a doctor, spent a night at Lodge's home after Lady Lodge had passed on. Sir Oliver was almost enthusiastic in the letter to Hill in which he referred to the sitting and the fingerprints of Walter, Margery's brother and guide, which were obtained. He also mentioned that fingerprints of his son Raymond were produced on the same occasion.

Lodge also sat with Eusapia Paladino, the Continental medium, who was much tested by psychic researchers and is frequently quoted by them. He is also reported to have sat with Helen Duncan, though I cannot find any detailed account of that sitting. Lodge's findings in his sitting with Eusapia were challenged by Dr Hodgson, of the S.P.R., and in most unsuitable circumstances test sittings were held with her at Cambridge.

This peculiar woman, who was uncannily sensitive to her surroundings, was reported to have cheated in the presence of several people who expected her to cheat. But Lodge was unshaken in his testimony and paid no attention to her character, for what he had seen he could not doubt. Years later, further sittings were carried out by men from the S.P.R., including a couple of conjurers, and they had striking results.

Lodge sat with Charles Richet, the French researcher, F. W. H. Myers and Dr Ochorowicz at Richet's house on the Ile Rabaud, in the Mediterranean, with Paladino as the medium. He writes of the séance: "However the facts are to be explained, the possibility of the facts I am constrained to admit; there is no further room in my mind for doubt. Any person without invincible prejudice who had had the same experience would come to the same broad conclusion, viz. that things hitherto held impossible do actually occur. If one such fact be plainly established, the conceivability of others may be more readily granted, and I concentrated my attention, namely on what seemed to me the most simple and definite thing; viz., the movement of an 'untouched object' in sufficient light for no doubt of its motion to exist. This I have now witnessed several times, the fact of movement being vouched for by both sight and hearing, sometimes also by touch, and the object of movement being demonstrated by the sounds heard by an outside observer and by permanent alteration in position of objects." Eusapia at this séance was strictly controlled, and it was after this that Lodge concurred in the view that the movements were caused by some protuberance drawn psychically from the medium's body.

I have already mentioned that he had, with his usual facility for analysis, observed that when ectoplasm was produced and manipulated by spirit operators, reactions could be observed on the body of the medium. He had, in his few experiences with materialisation mediums, noticed what Crawford of Belfast elaborated into a series of laws as definite as those of chemistry and physics. Lodge had clearly grasped the mode of operation of inspiration—from vague feelings to promptings and to classical examples like those mentioned in the Bible. He did not consider that he often had conscious intuitions, but I think he rightly suspected that in his case it operated through vivid dreams which he occasionally experienced. He records how one morning, when half awake, he dreamed that his son Raymond was in a big attack then going on, in the last war. He also says that he perceived "they" (spirit people) were taking care of him and he had this in mind before he read the morning papers in which he could see nothing that referred to his dream. It was at this time that he said he had hitherto held aloof from Spiritualist platforms because he held that his business at that time as a scientist was to investigate and establish, rather than to emotionalise over things.

It is almost a coincidence that at the same period he wrote a long letter to Hill in which he describes his view of death, "as a natural operation, certainly no worse than birth; and the transition itself seems to me merely interesting, not perturbing at all, if only surviving friends will not make a fuss and go on grieving as if some elaborate misfortune had happened to one." So much had his proof of Survival and his experiences with mediums prepared him for the blow that was about to fall, and of which he had an intuition in the vivid dream he had earlier described to his friend Hill. A few months later, his son Raymond was killed, and Lodge wrote of that with the same detachment, apparently, as he did of other things. But possibly it was to conceal his own feelings.

Always he was opposed to priests, for being of Noncomformist upbringing, he held the view that they dictated the views of their followers too much. In a summary of his opinion he showed that they were all naturally hostile to psychic investigation. He was sympathetic to Dr Crawford's work in Belfast, and even made suggestions along which lines he might work to check whether the fall in temperature noticed in physical phenomena could be due to molecular action, which also might explain how the table was lifted. Lodge, while on a visit to his friend Hill at Bradford, sat with the Yorkshire medium, Aaron Wilkinson, and about the same time he wrote to Hill giving his opinion of Feda, the spirit control of the medium, Mrs Osborne Leonard. His view is: "Concerning Feda, there is always the possibility that she, and her like, are secondary personalities.

But at any rate she is a personality, and one whom my family feel friendly towards. I don't know that it much matters whether she is a secondary or primary personality. I am inclined, however, to be guided by what they say on the Other Side about these things; they evidently treat these personalities as distinct people." How much Spiritualism meant to Lodge is shown by another letter written in May, 1918, when the husband of one of his daughters was killed while flying. Sir Oliver writes of his daughter's attitude: "She knows, as you say, that he is still with her in a sense, and already he has come through; Raymond brought him very quickly. He has sent excellent messages at an anonymous sitting which my daughter Norah had. Indeed, he controlled himself. Raymond was on the spot to receive him. There is much to tell you, but I can't now."

Lodge also experimented with apparatus for magnifying the direct voice. He was interested in Robert Blatchford's investigations into Spiritualism and his subsequent conviction. He wrote with gentle irony about the right wing of the Society for Psychical Research, whose President, he said, "had ridden the theory of telepathy to death." You can see in this that gradually Lodge was moving to the view where he regards the facts of Survival as fundamental, and that any public man or woman who becomes convinced after careful investigation is to be regarded as an acquisition and as an indication that thought is slowly moving.

To the very end he held to his belief in Survival, once denying an American rumour in these terms: "My conviction about survival is absolute, and not likely to be shaken. If the rumour arises rationally, and is not an invention of R.C.s, that is Roman Catholics, or some other unscrupulous party, it may ...."

Lodge was as brilliant an expositor of physics as he was of psychics, and he could tell an audience of 2000 people about the reality of the unseen things, such as molecules, atoms and electrons, as clearly as he could discourse on the unseen reality of things psychical. He could hold an audience of ordinary people spellbound by the clarity with which he explained some of the deeper things of science and Survival. He defended many kinds of mediumship and quoted experiences to explain his attitude.

He told the story of a diagnosis being given by a medium, Mrs Thompson, a poor woman who lived in a back street in Liverpool. She held a piece of cloth, and from that diagnosed pressure on the brain of the person from whom the material was obtained. She said that the pressure was caused by a piece of bone in a certain position. Lodge said that the famous surgeon who subsequently operated successfully was Sir Robert Jones. The injury was missed by the first doctor who attended the patient. Sir Oliver reported the case for the Society for Psychical Research, but they turned it down, he says, "quite unnecessarily."

This remarkable man, who endeared himself to ordinary people as no other scientist has done in this country, held firmly to his advocacy of Survival to the very end, saying that all that had changed was that he had received more and more evidence and that he was convinced that beings from the other world constantly strove to help people on this earth.

What did Lodge contribute to radio? He said that the true originators of radio were Maxwell and Hertz. Upon their work everyone built. He stated what we have already noticed, that his own main work was connected with the ether of space, and in a dispassionate discussion on the merits of Einstein's theory of relativity in contrast with his own, he showed that he was content, as a true scientist should be, to await the judgment of time. So far as I have been able to discover the question has not been decided. He did not regard his theory as inspired or authoritative and objectively discussed the merits of relativity. I mention this, not to confuse the ordinary reader or to impress him that I have a knowledge of scientific theory, which is not so, but merely to indicate the quality of the mind of Lodge, who had seized upon something which he regarded as fundamental, if proved, and as important as the principles of Newton. I do this to indicate the mettle of men who, having done these things, were convinced of the truth of Survival.

Lodge's other work, in his own words, was in his lecture on wireless in 1894, at the Royal Institution, and given later at the British Association, where it excited great interest. His friend, Alexander Muirhead, applied Lodge's discoveries to telegraphy. The Lodge-Muirhead syndicate was formed and was finally bought up by the Marconi company. Sir Oliver thought so much of Hertz that he wrote a book to his memory called *The Work of Hertz and his Successors.* Two years after Sir Oliver had developed his wireless discovery, Marconi took his development to a man called Preece, in charge of government telegraphs, who assisted him. Lodge's comment on Preece is that he "was far more ignorant than he ought to have been of what had already been done." Marconi overcame many practical difficulties, but he had the assistance of government officials, and commercialised a system of radio by the use of the Hertzian waves.

Lodge says, "The tuning however, which is now so essential, was begun by me in 1897; a patent which was extended by the courts, and was included in the sale of the Lodge-Muirhead syndicate to the Marconi Company. For the use of this patent, as I am mentioning a lot of things, I may mention that the Marconi Company pay me a thousand a year during its extended life; but as a matter of fact it has not much longer to live—only three or four years."

And there is the Lodge ignition system from which millions of motorists and aviators have benefited without realising to whom they were indebted. Lodge was indeed a benefactor of the human race.

CHAPTER FOURTEEN

"IMPOSSIBLE TO FIND A FLAW"

LODGE'S experiences of the mediumship of Margery Crandon of Boston led him to introduce Dr Robin J. Tillyard, chief entomologist to the Australian Government. Once as a test, Sir Oliver had two rings made of different kinds of wood, grown on his own estate. These he sent to Boston and, at a séance with Margery Crandon as the medium, and her brother Walter, as the guide, the rings were interlocked, a feat impossible without psychic aid if done in a genuine manner. Sir Oliver regarded this as a striking test, and the rings were kept in a case at the Crandon home for many years. But when Hannen Swaffer inspected them one day, he found that the rings were broken. He was of opinion that there is a law of frustration which works in all things, and that at this stage of the world's evolution it is not possible to have permanent physical proof of the reality of psychic laws and forces.

Lodge wrote to Dr Crandon, the medium's husband, of Tillyard's request: "He has an idea that it would diminish the opportunities for accusation of collusion if he were allowed a solitary sitting with Margery in a room arranged by himself, and thinks that if he got results under those conditions, the sceptics would be reduced to accusing him of collusion, which, considering his position as a scientific man, would be too absurd."

Crandon agreed, and the sitting took place at the home of a doctor who was not in any way associated with the Crandon circle. Dr Tillyard took charge of Margery's séance garments, which he thoroughly searched, as he did all the apparatus necessary for the production of thumbprints. He prepared the dental wax, which he marked. Margery was fixed in a chair with adhesive tape bandages which were tightly placed round her bare wrists, binding them to two arms of the chair, and around her stockinged ankles and then tied to the legs of the chair. All these bandages were marked by Tillyard with blue pencil, so that it would have been impossible for her to have moved either hands or feet without showing the change in position by the change in the blue pencil marks.

Three supernormal thumbprints were obtained. In his letter to Lodge, written a few hours after the sitting, Tillyard says: "It was by far the most wonderful séance I have ever attended. I think the arrangements which we made were scientifically severe, and at the same time put on record the most marvellous results in the whole history of psychic research. It seems to me quite impossible to find a single flaw in this wonderful result. This séance is, for me, the culminating point of all my psychical research. I can now say, if I so desire, 'nunc dimitis,' and go on with my own legitimate entomological work."

Tillyard wanted his scientific colleagues to know about this, probably his most important contribution to scientific knowledge, so he wrote to *Nature* a detailed account of this solus sitting and other séances. It was not published. In his last article, two years afterwards, he wrote, "As the result of further experiments with the remarkable Boston medium, Mrs L.R.G. Crandon, I feel that scientific proof of survival has at last been obtained." In describing these proofs he said: "The possibilities of fraud have been eliminated in two ways; by using such controls as the nature of each experiment clearly calls for if a charge of possible straight-out fraud is to be avoided; by devising experiments which, in their very nature, are either manifestly impossible to human beings in the flesh, or at any rate, impossible under the conditions of actual performance. The experiments can be repeated time after time, and the same results are obtained. The main proofs of survival obtained lie in phenomena which, whether of the so-called mental or physical type, are normally impossible of performance by human beings."

To him these séances proved conclusively that Walter, Margery's guide, was a real personality, independent of the medium, and of him he wrote: "Walter can handle delicate objects and place them accurately in the dark without doing any damage. He can select and cognise objects not known to any living person in the world, thus proving that he does not depend on telepathy or knowledge stored up in any person's subconscious mind. Finally, he can produce his thumbprints in dental wax in the dark more quickly than an ordinary man can do them in the light. My own conclusion is that Walter Stinson, who died in 1912, has fully proved in a scientific manner his claim that his personality has survived physical death."

In the same issue of *Nature* in which that article appeared a leading article was published pooh-poohing all that Tillyard had written. It said, "We ourselves preserve an open mind towards work for the advancement of knowledge and the acquisition of truth in all spheres of intellectual activity." Although *Nature* could not suggest that Tillyard had behaved unscientifically, it said, "Once it is proved that a spirit can mould a larynx and mouth cavity out of ectoplasm, and can force air through them so as to make sound and speech by such means, it would be easy to accept most of the other supernormal phenomena to which Dr Tillyard has given attention." Yet these, and many other things, Tillyard proved. The nature of *Nature* is beyond understanding.

CHAPTER FIFTEEN

"ABSURD BUT TRUE"

CHARLES RICHET, a famous French physiologist, investigated psychic phenomena during his long life, though he wrestled violently in a conflict between the materialism to which his profession gave rise and the evidence he received. In the end he had to admit that he was convinced of Survival. It is perhaps a tragedy that his admission was made only a few weeks before he passed on. He wrote to his Italian friend, Professor Ernesto Bazzano, admitting that he was convinced. This, after 30 years of doubt and scepticism, showed that it was no whim and that his acceptance was not reached after a bereavement. Describing the phenomenon of materialisation he once said, "It is absurd but true." He meant, of course, it was absurd in the sense that the physiologist would use it; that either it contradicted his theories or did not run parallel to the laws of physiology with which he was familiar. Intellectuals, when they come into this field of research, are nearly always concerned to find what they call a "parallel," that is to say, they seek to find in the laws governing psychic phenomena laws similar to those which govern the phenomena of this physical world.

Richet, more than ten years before he admitted that he was convinced, said in the course of a discussion with Sir Oliver Lodge on Survival: "To what then is the spiritistic hypothesis in opposition? First of all, very briefly, there is physiology, that is to say a very precise science, rich in demonstrations which have established by innumerable proofs a narrow, rigorous, parallelism between intellectual function—otherwise called memory and the brain. ...For myself, without being able to give a firm demonstration (for one cannot prove a negative), I cannot believe that memory can exist without the anatomical and physiological integrity of the brain. Whenever there is no more oxygen, whenever the temperature is too high or low, when there are a few drops of atrophine or morphine or chloroform introduced into the blood, whenever the course of cerebral irrigation is stopped—memory alters and disappears. Spiritists cannot deny these facts."

Even Richet was mistaken. Mediumship proves that life, consciousness and memory survive the interruption of cerebral irrigation to the point where the brain decays and the body is uninhabitable. The dead can, at the "absurd but true" materialisation séances, fashion for themselves, out of the living structure of ectoplasm, vehicles through which memory is expressed.

They give facts of their own lives, speak in their voices to prove their identity by recalling incidents not only of their own past life, but of the daily occupations of those to whom they seek to bring the conviction that eluded Richet for so long, because his cerebral channels were irrigated by a mental bloodstream influenced by the unwillingness to accept facts.

The story of Richet's final admission is touching. For long he had corresponded with Bozzano, even after he had experimented with extra-sensory perception, and even when he had discovered that telepathy could be, in his opinion, related to clairvoyance. Bozzano wrote this letter to a friend, Miss E. Maude Bubb: "I was pleased to hear that you had sent an extract of my letter to you to *Psychic News* in which I told you that Professor Richet, in the last months of his life, had acknowledged the acceptance of a belief in Spiritualism. I gladly consent to send you a copy of the letter in which he announced the joyful news. This is what took place. As a mark of appreciation he presented me with his book *Au Secours*, in which he had written the following inscription, 'To my learned and valiant friend, E. Bozzano, in complete, increasing sympathy.' As he had underlined the word 'increasing,' I was surprised and delighted, for it flashed into my mind that such emphasis given to the word must have a theoretical importance of more than mere personal appreciation. I could not refrain from mentioning this to Professor Richet, telling him with some diffidence of the hopes which that underlined word had kindled in my breast. He replied in a letter on the corner of which was written in large letters, and underlined, 'Confidential.' He began the letter by commenting on a remark of mine about the difficult question as to whether there be 'relative free will conditioned by a circumscribed fate which controls our life.' " This is the letter he sent to Bozzano:

"My dear and eminent colleague and friend, I am in complete agreement with you. I do not believe in that simple explanation whereby the events of our life and the sequences of our existence are due solely to chance; although one cannot prove it. There is a Fate, that is to say a force, which guides us and which leads us where it will by strange and tortuous paths. Even apart from the guidance of our life, there are such striking coincidences that it is difficult not to see in them something like a purpose. (Whose purpose or what purpose?) And now I'm going to speak to you quite confidentially: What you alleged is true. What neither Myers, nor Hodgson, nor Hyslop, nor Sir Oliver Lodge were able to do, you have accomplished by your masterly monographs, which I read with an almost religious fervour. They form a strange contrast to the murky theories which obscure our science. Accept, I pray, my sentiments of appreciation and gratitude."

Richet is a classic instance of the struggle of the honest materialist who is striving to resist the evidence for Spiritualism. In 1927, when the French review *Comœdia* printed a series on the views of eminent scientists on the survival of the soul, Richet made this contribution: "I am going to answer you with absolute frankness. Sometimes I believe. Sometimes (more often, perhaps) I do not believe. How can a physiologist conceive that there can be a survival of consciousness without a brain? On the other hand, how deny the facts called spiritistic which by hypothesis support a more simple explanation than any other?"

That is the confession, the honest confession, of a soul in its pilgrimage towards a great truth. He was not alone. There are many, among them those who have received an abundance of proof, who in their darker moments doubt what they know and seek to find an alternative explanation. It is a common activity of the human soul and is not confined to scientists. Richet wrote to Bozzano "in most appreciative homage. From a seeker of long standing, but one still on the threshold." After this he admitted Bozzano had convinced him. Of the materialisation which prompted him to say of it that it was "absurd but true," he wrote many years before: "To admit the reality of these phenomena was to me actual pain; but to ask a physiologist, a physicist or a chemist to admit that a form that has a circulation of blood, warmth and muscles, that exhales carbonic acid, has weight, speaks and thinks, can issue from a human body is to ask of him an intellectual effort that is really painful."

That was one way of admitting, however reluctantly, a fact.

Then after a sitting with Eva C., he wrote of a materialisation: "It walks, speaks, moves and breathes like a human being. Its body is resistant and has a certain muscular strength. It is neither a lay figure nor a doll, nor an image reflected by a mirror; it is as a living being; it is as a living man; and there are reasons for resolutely setting aside every other supposition than one or the other of these two hypotheses; either that of a phantom having the attributes of life; or that of a living person playing the part of a phantom."

To prove that the materialisation was not caused by "a living person playing the part of a phantom," he held the sittings behind locked doors, and while the materialised form was in sight the medium was seen in the cabinet. There was a rumour that there was a trap door in the room. Richet not only examined the floor minutely but obtained from the architect of the building a certificate to the effect that there was no trap door. At another sitting Richet was given permission to cut six inches of hair from the head of a materialised form. This hair was unlike that of the medium and was fine, silky and undyed. Microscopical examination showed it to be real hair.

Bozzano's comment on Richet's admission that he accepted Survival as the explanation of the psychic phenomena, was: "It is to me a comforting thought that in the end I was the victor, for Richet died convinced of the fact of survival; but he was only convinced during the last few months and this was effected by means of my latest articles in *La Ricerca Psychica*, " (an Italian psychic journal which Richet read assiduously).

Bozzano was a specialist in the study of haunting. Another Italian scientist interested in poltergeists and hauntings was Cesare Lombroso. He is one of many Italian and French savants who experimented extensively with Eusapia Paladino. His attention was called to her by another professor, but Lombroso did not sit with her until 1891, when he was immediately convinced and wrote, "I am filled with confusion and regret that I combated with so much persistence the possibility of the facts called Spiritualistic."

I think that the further we travel from the psychic experiments of British and American scientists and pass to the Continent of Europe, we become involved in theories, not to explain the phenomena, but to explain them away, nearly always on a basis of materialism, One of the outstanding examples was Baron von Schrenck-Notzing, a Munich doctor who spent years in experiments with Eva Carriere, called by researchers "Eva C." As a result he wrote one of the largest tomes in the history of psychic research, and one of the dullest. Some of the many photographs in his well-named monumental work, *Phenomena of Materialisation,* are grotesque and meaningless. Others are striking in their evidence for the reality of psychic gifts possessed by Eva Carriere which were not of the highest order. It is difficult to see how they could be, for the baron was wholly unsympathetic towards Spiritualism, as he revealed by this statement: "I am of the opinion that the hypothesis of spirits not only fails to explain the least detail of these processes, but in every way it obstructs and shackles serious scientific research."

This must be contrasted with the broad outlook of men like Lodge, Barrett, Crookes, Crawford, Hare and others. The baron was convinced that what they had done was not "serious scientific research," for he says in the introduction to his tome: "It is not without some misgiving that I publish in the present work the results of four years' observations of the medium, Eva C. For the observations of mediumistic phenomena hitherto made, do not, up to now, in spite of their continuity and independent agreement, and in spite of the high reputation of the authors whose names vouch for facts stated, fulfil the requirements of an exact scientific method. This may, however, be due to the factor of the occurrences themselves."

Even this narrow-minded investigator had his troubles, for he had to combat the hatred and suspicion, powerful on the Continent, of those who were opposed to psychic research of any kind, for he says: "As to the means sometimes adopted by those who wish to prove the supposed fraud underlying mediumistic phenomena, the experience of the author furnishes an instructive contribution. Convinced that the author was the victim of expert deceptions practised by two women, that is, the medium Eva C and her protectress Madame Bisson, somebody secretly and without the author's knowledge instructed a well-known Parisian detective office to watch these two ladies. The employees of the firm, besides gathering the necessary information about the medium herself, also gained illegal possession of a number of photographic copies of the negatives obtained during the experiments, though these were the exclusive property of the author and his collaborators. In spite of the unwelcome annoyances to which those two ladies were exposed by the tool of this anonymous agency, not only in the street but in their domestic and family life for eight months, the agency did not succeed in furnishing evidence of fraud or in finding the firm which supplied what they supposed to be the material required for the sitting, in the way of hand shapes of all kinds, of veils, muslins, plaster casts of faces, or portrait drawings of four entire phantom images."

He describes the activities of the private detectives as a "miserable fiasco." In the end, the baron finished pretty much as he began, without understanding mediumship, for he wanted to have everything under his control while it is very natural that the people on the Other Side, with whom the mediums co-operated, wanted conditions which they knew to be the best for the production of phenomena.

To Schrenck-Notzing also, mediumship was a problem, and not an activity of the soul working in co-operation with beings who no longer inhabit the physical body. None of the photographs he obtained can in any way compare with results in England or America, and the explanation is not hard to find. In Schrenck-Notzing's experiments, one doctor tried to grab a materialised form and naturally failed, leaving the medium in considerable pain. It was Schrenck-Notzing who regretted that, in his own experiments, some of the materialisations bore such a strong resemblance to the dead people whose spirits they claimed to be.

CHAPTER SIXTEEN

SCIENCE CLOSES ITS MIND

SIR WILLIAM FLETCHER BARRETT, who was Professor of Experimental Physics at the Royal College of Science, Dublin, for 37 years, had his struggles with the orthodox scientists of his day because of his interest in psychic research and Spiritualism. As in the case of all the scientists quoted in this book, Barrett began his inquiries, not because of personal grief, nor in the declining years of old age, but as a matter of professional curiosity which led him to consider trance, telepathy and, later, physical phenomena. He was among the followers of the Society for Psychical Research, but differs from many researchers in his breadth of mind and tolerance.

He started his researches a year after his appointment at Dublin and within two years he submitted a paper to be read before the British Association. The Biological Committee refused it and the anthropological sub-section accepted it only on the casting vote of the chairman, Alfred Russel Wallace. This paper expressed Barrett's view on telepathy which he had proved experimentally. He was a scientific Rationalist in that he held firmly that inquirers into nature should be bold in framing theories, dispassionate in testing them and eager to discard them when once they are disproved, or are incapable of explaining all the facts being considered. He discarded his theories one by one as the evidence marched into his consciousness as a result of experiments in séances. At one time he held that the evidence obtained by Sir William Crookes and Professor de Morgan, the mathematician, could have been attributed to mal-observation and hallucination. This view was shattered by events.

An English solicitor of repute, whom he described as Mr C., rented a friend's house not far from his own at Kingsdown, Co. Dublin. Barrett discovered that this man had a mediumistic child aged ten. The family were not Spiritualists, and at first thought the child was playing tricks when raps were heard in all kinds of circumstances. Barrett began his investigation in the home of Mr C. on a bright sunny morning while seated round a large dining-table. Soon they heard a scraping sound, followed by raps on the table and on the backs of the chairs while the child's hands and feet were closely watched. She did not stir. The sounds grew louder, imitating the noise of hammering nails into wood until Barrett thought there must be carpenters working above. He investigated. There was no one in the room above. The raps grew stronger, and when a cheerful song was struck up by the sitters, or when music was played, the raps kept time to the music in what he describes as "a most amusing way." The raps changed to a loud rhythmic scraping as though the bow of a 'cello were being drawn across a piece of wood. The physicist put his ear to the spot when this sound emanated and distinctly felt the rhythmic vibration in the table but could see no cause above or below it to explain the phenomena.

He asked raps to be produced on a small table near him, one that the child was not touching, and raps were heard. He put one hand above the table, one hand below, and as the raps were repeated in the space enclosed between his hands, he felt the slight jarring noise made by each sound. Messages were spelt out through the alphabet, and it was later found that a child was the communicator, for childish spelling errors were made. For weeks this investigation went on. Sometimes furniture was moved. Once a huge mahogany dining-table, large enough to seat 12 people, rose off the floor sufficiently to enable him to put his foot beneath a castor. When Barrett tried to lift the table afterwards, he found that with all his strength he could move it only with difficulty.

He tested the current theory to explain away rappings—that they were caused by slipping the toe or knee joints partially in and out with a click. He asked the child to put her hands flat on a wall while he did the same, then both stretched their legs as far from the wall as possible, pretending it was a new kind of game. While the serious professor and the ten year-old-child were standing in this acrobatic pose, in which muscular movement of the limbs was ruled out, the raps were heard in the room, the child was motionless and the professor was still. Only the professor and the girl were in the room, and to Barrett's satisfaction he concluded that she was a genuine medium. And she was only ten. It would almost appear that this evidence was arranged by invisible agents for Barrett, for when the family returned to England, the phenomena gradually died away. At no time had the communications exceeded the frivolous, although the little girl was discovered to have been holding nightly talks with some invisible companion who spelt out messages rapidly by the alphabet.

Barrett's next sittings were with a Miss Lauder, who lived with a relative, a prominent Dublin photographer. All the sittings were held in gaslight sufficient to enable Barrett to see what was happening. Once he was startled when, sitting at the table, loud raps were heard. Then with his hand out of sight of the others, he asked the unseen operator to say how many fingers he held out. The correct number was given twice, and knocks were given in answer to his request while all the sitters took their hands from the table. Then, while the hands and feet of all were clearly visible, and no one was touching the table, it sidled about in an uneasy manner.

"It was a four-legged table, some four feet square," he says, "and heavy. In obedience to my request, first the two legs nearest me and then the two hinder legs rose eight or ten inches completely off the ground and thus remained a few moments; not a person touched the table the whole time. I withdrew my chair further and the table then moved towards me—Mr and Miss L not touching the table at all—finally the table came up to the armchair in which I sat and imprisoned me in my seat. When thus under my very nose the table rose repeatedly, and it enabled me to be perfectly sure, by the evidence of touch, that it was quite off the ground and that no human being had any part in this or the other movements. To suppose that the table was moved by invisible and non-existent threads worked by an imaginary accomplice, who must have floated in the air unseen, is a conjecture which sceptics are at liberty to make if they choose."

At a sitting in his own house, which Miss Lauder had not visited before, raps, ticks and loud percussive sounds were heard in good daylight. Then suddenly, while the tips of their fingers only rested on the table, the heavy piece of furniture at which they sat began to prance and became so violent that he had to stop the sitting to prevent the chandelier in the room below being damaged. Afterwards he tried to imitate the movements of the table and found it could be done only by using both hands and all his strength. That ended his theory of hallucination and mal-observation.

Barrett attended with Crawford a sitting of the Goligher circle. He sat outside the small family circle. The room was illuminated with a bright gas flame burning in a lantern, with a large red glass window, on the mantelpiece. The room was small and as his eyes became accustomed to the light he saw all the sitters clearly. They sat round a small table with hands joined together, but no one touching the table. Very soon knocks came and messages were spelt out as one of them. repeated the alphabet aloud. "Suddenly the knocks increased in violence," wrote Barrett, "and being encouraged, a tremendous bang came which shook the room and resembled the blow of a sledgehammer on an anvil. A tin trumpet, which had been placed below the table, now poked out its smaller end close under the top of the table near where I was sitting. I was allowed to try and catch it, but it dodged all my attempts in the most amusing way, the medium on the opposite side sat perfectly still while at my request all held up their joined hands so that I could see no one was touching the trumpet, as it played peep-bo with me.

"Sounds, like the sawing of wood, the bouncing of a ball and other noises occurred, which were inexplicable. Then the table began to rise from the floor some eighteen inches and remained so suspended and quite level. I was allowed to go up to the table and saw clearly no one was touching it, a clear space separating the sitters from the table. I tried to press the table down, and though I exerted all my strength, could not do so; then I climbed up on the table and sat on it, my feet off the floor, when I was swayed to and fro and finally tipped off. The table of its own accord now turned upside down; no one touching it, and I tried to lift it off the ground, but it could not be stirred. It appeared screwed to the floor. At my request all the sitters' clasped hands had been kept raised above their heads, and I could see that no one was touching the table; when I desisted from trying to lift the inverted table from the floor it righted itself again of its own accord, no one helping it. Numerous sounds displaying an amused intelligence the P. came, and after each individual present had been greeted with some farewell raps the sitting ended."

That is the testimony of a famous scientist, but he was not deceived into thinking that his words or his evidence would make any appreciable difference to public opinion, or that his statements would be more impressive than those of other investigators. In this he showed the detachment and humility of an inquirer after truth.

Barrett had a curious experience in psychic photography. A friend, whom he describes as Lady C., rented for the summer Lord Combermere's country house, Combermere Abbey, Cheshire. Lady C. admired the fine panelled library so much that she wanted a photograph of it. She focused her camera on a space fronting an empty carved oak armchair on which Lord Combermere formerly sat. She took a plate from a new box in the darkroom, loaded it into the slide and made the exposure. She was startled when, on developing the plate, she saw sitting in the oak armchair, a legless old man. Not long afterwards, they found that Lord Combermere had died as a result of an accident in London, and at the moment the photograph was being taken his body was being buried in the family vault a few miles from his country house. This coincidence was revealed only after the plate was developed and led to arguments whether the psychic extra on the plate resembled the dead peer.

Barrett was told about this and he wrote to the Combermere family, sending them a picture for identification. On the whole it was agreed, that while the likeness was not good, the figure was seated in an attitude common to Lord Combermere. Barrett inquired of Lady C., who had taken the picture, and she told him that the exposure lasted 15 minutes and that for a brief time she was out of the room. The scientist thought a servant might have walked in, sat down in the chair and hurried out when he heard Lady C. returning. So Barrett exposed a photographic plate in the panelled library at a friend's house where he was staying. He asked the eldest son, a young man, to walk into the room, sit down in the oak armchair, cross and uncross his legs, move his head slightly, and then walk out. When the plate was developed, it was a duplicate of the Combermere picture, for a shadowy, aged man, legless, was sitting in the chair and there were no signs of anyone having entered or left the room. The Combermeres had questioned members of the family to see whether they had entered the room in which Lady C. had taken her picture, but they had not.

After Barrett had published his account, one of Combermere's relatives wrote and told him of something she had not previously known, saying: "You say he had not lost his legs, but he died from an accident in which they were so much injured he could never have used them again. He was run over by a wagon at Knightsbridge, crossing the street, and only lived a few weeks. Lord Combermere was my father-in-law and I lived some years at the Abbey with him. I was much interested in the written account of the photograph. The face was always too indistinct to be quite convincing to me, though some of his children had no doubt at all of his identity. I may add, none of the men servants in the house in the least resembled the figure and were all young men; whilst the outside men were all attending the funeral, which was taking place at the church four miles off, at the very time the photograph was being done."

Barrett probably knew as much as any scientist about the divining rod on which he wrote authoritatively, and he carried out successful experiments to test Reichenbach's views on lights which he said emanated from the poles of a magnet. He did this by secreting a magnet in a room and inviting sensitives to sit in total darkness and describe what they saw. Later he asked them to draw what they had seen, and all the drawings tallied.

With approval he quoted Professor de Morgan's view: "The Spiritualists, beyond a doubt, are in the track that has led to all advancement in physical science; their opponents are the representatives of those who have striven against progress ... I say the deluded spirit rappers are on the right track; they have the spirit and method of the grand old times when those paths were cut through the uncleared forests in which it is now the daily routine to walk. What was that spirit? It was the spirit of universal examination, wholly unchecked by fear of being detected in the investigation of nonsense." With further approval he quoted de Morgan comparing Spiritualists with Newton, in that they had—and have—the courage to experiment ceaselessly on the basis of a revolutionary hypothesis, and added, what is well known, that what was the improbable wild speculation of yesterday is the orthodox belief of science of tomorrow.

Barrett also had experiences with the ouija board in a small private circle of friends and writes that they found that even when the sitters were blindfolded evidential messages were still spelt out. Once he took the place of a sitter and was securely blindfolded, with the result: "On putting my fingers on the indicator, along with the two other sitters, the extraordinary vigour, decision and swiftness with which the indicator moved startled me, and it seemed incredible that any coherent message could be in process of delivery. But the recorder had taken down the message which came as follows: 'The same combination must always work together in order to obtain the important messages, as it is very tiring unless the same three are present; there is one present who is unsuited for the receiving.'" The unsuitable person was Barrett.

He had experience of a non-professional medium who wrote automatic messages upside down, as though someone was sitting opposite her, controlling her hand. Some of the communications came from a dead brother to whom the medium was deeply attached, and others from a friend. This is one of the communications written in this strange upside-down writing: "I saw the earth lying dark and cold under the stars in the first beginning of the wintry sunrise. It was the landscape I knew so well and had looked at so often. Suddenly sight was born to me; my eyes became open. I saw the spiritual world dawn upon the actual, like the blossoming of a flower. For this I have no words. Nothing I could say would make any of you comprehend the wonder of that revelation, but it will be yours in time.

I was drawn as if by affinity to the world which is now mine. But I am not fettered there. I am much drawn to earth, but by no unhappy chain. I am drawn to those I love; to the places much endeared."

This mediumship impressed Barrett, who had investigated nearly every kind of phenomena. He was in communication with scientists in various countries and wrote a good deal about the evidence they had obtained. He was so deeply interested in promoting research, that at the end of his book, *On the Threshold of the Unseen*, he has suggestions for experimenters, and includes advice from Stainton Moses on the conduct of a circle.

After an extensive inquiry into dowsing in which he demonstrated the accuracy of the dowsers he wrote: "The sudden twisting of the twig, even the violent breaking of one branch of it, upon attempting to restrain its gyration, is an involuntary act. It is true that cultured men of scientific tastes who are dowsers, like Dean Ovenden, utterly deny this explanation of its sudden motion and believe an unknown force of some kind is the true cause; but, if so, it must be an external force of which we have not the remotest conception. The chief question, however, is the nature of the faculty which leads a good dowser to discover the hidden spring or metallic ore when other means have failed. The explanation, I believe, is not physical but psychical. All the evidence points to the fact that the good dowser subconsciously possesses the faculty of clairvoyance."

How much Barrett thought of Spiritualism and the practice of communication with the dead is seen in the dedication of that book to his wife, which reads, "To the dear memory of one whose radiant faith gave her 'the assurance of things hoped for,' and needed not the evidence of things unseen which this book may possibly give to some stricken souls and other seekers after truth."

CHAPTER SEVENTEEN

THE MORAL TO BE DRAWN

THERE are many scientists, psychologists and others who have investigated mediumship and proved by their writings and speeches, when taken in total and examined carefully, that Spiritualism is true. What do we mean by Spiritualism? That belief in the personal survival of bodily death which is proved by mediums who, in the exercise of their spiritual gifts in cooperation with discarnate beings, pass communications between this world and the next. That is but the beginning, and we have not progressed far from the initial stages. I think that it was never intended by the great organisation on the Other Side, in whose charge is this vast system of communication, that there should be continuous laboratory experiments concerned only with the mechanics of certain phases of phenomena to the detriment of the living and warm evidence that man lives beyond the grave. If it were the intention of the skilful beings who, in less than a hundred years, have proved their case millions of times and still go on doing it, that there should be any one striking instance of proof which would stand for all time, then that would have been done.

Evidence grows as the consciousness of man expands; knowledge increases as he evolves; and new powers come to him as his morality is extended to cover not only himself and his country, but all races and all kingdoms of nature. When such reforming ideas are ignored, neglected or deliberately defied, the experiments become as crude and unsatisfactory as the apparitions of Munich in which Schrenck-Notzing delighted. But when there is a single-minded desire to allow the facts to prove themselves, we have the flowering of evidence of the kind produced in the presence of Crookes and Crawford, Hare and Zöllner. I have been told, and I accept it, that phases of mediumship vary with the times and are developed to suit the needs of the countries in which they are manifest. This in itself is a kind of psychic phenomenon, because it implies prevision and planning, for it takes a long time to develop a satisfactory medium.

Those scientists, whose works are here summarised, rendered a great service to humanity when they risked their reputations and gave their time to the study of things, not only opposed in their own days, but which were considered to be detrimental to all who partook of them. Each scientist in turn was accused of insanity, but only so far as his evidence for Spiritualism was concerned. No man is considered insane when he holds an orthodox opinion or seeks to destroy those who advocate new ideas. A dispassionate inquirer from another planet would be startled if told that there existed in this world so large a body of evidence for the facts of Survival, and that it had not found a way into the schools and universities. But in spite of that, this idea of Spiritualism, this practice of Spiritualism, has grown until it has permeated all classes of people and all kinds of thought.

The aim in collecting this evidence is not to strike dumb with amazement but to excite wonder, to stimulate curiosity, and to advance interest until people find for themselves whether this thing be true or false for them, for assuredly it has been proved to myriads of others on this planet. If all the personal traits of all mediums, if all the idiosyncrasies of all the researchers are laid on one side, if all the heat of the many controversies is allowed for, the solid substantial evidence remains and is testified to by a brilliant array of men honoured in their own countries and abroad.

Spiritualism cannot be contained in any laboratory; it cannot be made into a creed; it cannot be fashioned to suit any of the existing orthodoxies. It is a living fact always in advance of the knowledge of the day. New truths, new horizons of enlightenment are discovered only as men advance in the scale of evolution. Decade by decade, the world takes a diminishingly materialistic view of the universe. To this outlook, Spiritualism has contributed, I contend, much the larger proportion. A good deal has been done by scientists, especially physicists, who have extended the vision of their generations until now explanations of the operations of laws and the behaviour of matter are thought to reside and operate, not on this earth, but in regions beyond it.

The discoveries of the scientists percolate but slowly through to the masses of the people with whom Spiritualism is concerned. It is a truth for the million and not for the chosen minority. What can be demonstrated in the laboratory is not always possible in the home circle, and what is done in the home circle often transcends the happenings in the laboratory. For where love and kindness are the moving forces, communion between this world and the next becomes easier and better, and the results of a more striking order than when the aim is only cold and analytical research. It is difficult to induce a whole world to take an interest in a new scientific theory. It is a comparatively simple matter to capture the attention of the multitude by proof of survival beyond the grave for all men die.

This is the larger view, the wider concept, into which the body of scientific evidence here quoted must fall and find its proper place. The scientist, a pioneer in knowledge, must not be exalted above all other seekers after truth, for he who brings comfort to the mourning widow and the grieving child, he who can lift darkness from a troubled mind, he who can clear the vision and sharpen the desire to serve, he is indeed a greater servant of humanity. The humblest medium, who gives evidence of the continued existence and love of one who has passed out of the physical body to another who seeks the assurance of his presence, can take comfort from the works of great scientists and feel that service is founded on truth and can be demonstrated in a manner beyond the hopes of any creed ever invented to darken the minds of men.

Facts belong to no party and are contained in no dogma. Mankind is one and all races have common needs. Those who have proof of the power of the spirit require no words of mine; those who have evidence of the survival of those they love, need no assurance from me. But those who are in need, those who suffer, those who are in sorrow or any other adversity, can be assured, as science has shown, that there is a world beyond this filled with vibrant beings, men, women and children like themselves, willing to give all they have earned in the service of a mankind that often has been blind but more often misled into thinking that there is no life beyond the grave, and that the hopes expressed by teachers in all ages were vain.

At some time, we all have pondered this question of Survival. The difficulty is to find the knowledge that leads to the first step. Much is recorded and much has been made clear. The traffic of communicators between this world and the next grows, and it is not likely that, with all the service that has been rendered in the past, there shall be any diminution in the future. For truth does not grow less but increases by service. Though each man may do a little in this great cause, he does not know how much he achieves. One sows and many reap.

THE END

www.ingramcontent.com/pod-product-compliance
Lightning Source LLC
LaVergne TN
LVHW051631080426
835511LV00016B/2281